Johnny Cash

AN AMERICAN LEGEND

By Michael McCall

Edited by Nicholas Maier

American Media, Inc.

JOHNNY CASH
An American Legend

Copyright © 2003 AMI Books, Inc.

Cover design: Carlos Plaza
Interior design: Debbie Browning
Copy editor: Amy Persenaire

ISBN: 1-932270-32-9

First printing: December 2003

Printed in the United States of America

10 9 8 7 6 5 4 3 2 1

1

Johnny Cash was writing his own epitaph during his final years. In song after song, Cash cast his own life in stark relief. There were songs of salvation and deliverance, songs of death and decay and songs of allegory about a life both glorious and full of sin.

As if on cue, the legendary singer participated in a final music video that evocatively looked back at his life while displaying, with brutal and unadorned honesty, the ravages that age and illness had brought upon his body and his surroundings.

The video, Cash's cover of the Nine Inch Nails' song *Hurt*, put Cash among the nominees for the MTV Video Music Awards in August 2003 and among the leaders on the nomination list for the Country Music Association Awards in November. Even in his final months, Cash was still crossing genres, still garnering attention from both the rock and the country crowds. It was an appropriate ending for a man who blurred boundaries for his entire artistic life.

All of this creativity, the songs and the images, also revealed that one constant continued to run through Cash's art: He was a dignified man unafraid to be himself, a groundbreaker who fearlessly delved into the most tender areas of human existence and a master of his form who, from his first song to his last, bravely revealed all of his flaws while still standing tall and proud.

The video, directed by Mark Romanek, laid out Cash's life and his strengths as an artist as plainly and provocatively as possible. The song, written by rocker Trent Reznor, graphically describes drug abuse and how addiction separates and isolates individuals from the world and the ones they love. Undoubtedly, Cash related with that message; he nearly killed himself in the

1960s because of an addiction to amphetamines and he continued to battle substance abuse throughout his life.

"They're very sinister," he said of the "drug demon" and the "sex demon" in a *Rolling Stone* interview in 2002. "You got to watch them. They'll sneak up on you. All of a sudden there'll be a beautiful little Percodan laying there, and you'll want it."

Hurt begins with Cash strumming a black acoustic guitar and singing the volatile first lines: *"I hurt myself today, to see if I still feel."* By the time the couplet ended, the camera closed in tight on Cash's face. For those who hadn't seen him in recent years, the image was startling. His face had become disfigured, ravaged by age, illness and more than 34 surgeries on a broken jaw that pained him for the final decade of his life.

"What have I become?" Cash asked in the song. *"Everyone that I know goes away in the end."*

As Cash sang of needles and the damage they do, the video alternated between recent shots and film footage culled from his past. We see the elderly singer inside his ornately decorated home in Hendersonville, Tennessee, surrounded by photos of his mother Carrie Cash and framed pictures of an imposing Cash with his wife June Carter Cash in younger days.

We see video of him in his robust prime. We

see a striking, charismatic Man in Black on a train. We see him on stage in a prison concert. We see him walking along Old Hickory Lake, hiking with his son John Carter Cash on his vast rural property. We see him peering in a window of his tiny, weathered childhood home in Kingsland, Arkansas.

The contrast between now and then couldn't be more striking. Echoing a theme that ran through his music over the years, the video's images portray how even the proudest and most accomplished of humans withers against the onslaught of age and impending death.

Written by a young rocker, the lyrics to *Hurt* took on a different meaning when sung by this septuagenarian deity, this country King Lear. Reznor's song originally portrayed an addict broken and full of regret. But coming from Cash the lyrics showed a man painfully reflecting upon a noble life fraught with more than its share of vice and transgressions.

"I wear this crown of thorns, upon my liar's chair, full of broken thoughts I cannot repair," he sings and the connection to the life he's lived, this life of sin and salvation, is unmistakable.

The video received raves as soon as it was introduced. CMT, the country music cable channel, put it in heavy rotation — an ironic move, since mainstream country broadcasters had long ago turned their backs on one of its main heroes. The songs Cash created during his '90s comeback were heralded by the press and embraced by rock 'n' rollers, but country music considered the sounds of the Man in Black to be too dark and too raw for the polished, peppy image that radio endorsed.

But CMT couldn't resist. The video was too strong, the fan reaction too fervent, for the station not to highlight it daily. As young CMT host Katie Cook said in first introducing it, *Hurt* was "an artful new video that captures the 71-year-old icon at his most vulnerable."

The station also had two rock singers with country connections speak about *Hurt* as a way of confirming its hipness — despite the bleak aspects of the footage.

"It really played on all my fears about aging," Sheryl Crow said in a CMT news report. "Not about who he's become, but about the sweetness of life and the simplicity and the innocence that's lost. You see some of that early footage and, to me, that takes me back to a time that's far simpler. He's always been who he is. He's never changed who he was for any kind of popularity. He's always been the Man in Black — introspective, outspoken, fiery, do-or-die. And you see him and he's still that person."

Kid Rock, who was regularly featured in a

video on CMT singing his duet *Picture* with Sheryl Crow, also offered his reaction to *Hurt*. "He's one of the pillars of the foundation that holds up the music we all play today, in my eyes," said Kid. "To see that video absolutely moved me. It made me smile, it made me want to cry at times. It just absolutely touched me like no video can."

The video — and the self-eulogy it provided — was mentioned in all the front-page news stories the day after Cash died. He passed away at Nashville's Baptist Hospital at 1 a.m. Sept. 12 due to respiratory failure. "Johnny died due to complications from diabetes, which resulted in respiratory failure," his longtime manager Lou Robin said in a statement. "I hope friends and fans of Johnny will pray for the Cash family to find comfort during this very difficult time."

2

Cash spent his last years in and out of hospitals. The day prior to his death, he was released from Baptist Hospital after a three-week stay for treatment of a stomach ailment. He was forced to cancel his plans to travel to New York to appear on the MTV Video Music Awards. When he left the hospital, he spoke of returning to California to finish work on an album that was nearly complete. He also told the Country Music

Association that he wanted to attend its awards show in November in Nashville.

His career spanned nearly 50 years, reaching beyond songwriting, recording and concert appearances to include acting and writing books. During his career, he recorded more than 1,500 songs and released more than 140 singles. He drew songs freely from every genre of music, never limiting himself by style or form. But he also always insisted that he be known as one thing: a country music artist.

Death was a primary topic of his last several recordings. For "American IV: The Man Comes Around," the final album of original material released in his lifetime, Cash opened with a spoken passage: "And I heard, as it were, the noise of thunder, one of the four beasts saying, come and see, and I saw, and behold a white horse."

Obviously, the arrival of the reaper was ripe on his mind. In the title cut, which follows, Cash addressed the visitation, dealing with it in Biblical allegory. *"There's a man going 'round taking names, and he decides who to free and who to blame,"* Cash sings over a brittle, driving acoustic guitar. *"Everybody won't be treated all the same. There'll be a golden ladder reaching down, when the man comes around."*

By song's end, he's speaking in apocalyptic

terms, *"Whoever is unjust, let him be unjust still,"* Cash sings, his weak voice ominous and gaining power. *"Whoever is righteous, let him be righteous still. Whoever is filthy, let him be filthy still. Listen to the words long written down, when the man comes around."*

The album ends on a breezier but just as prophetic of a note. Singing in an uncharacteristic, lighthearted tone over a Dixieland-flavored backing track, Cash presents an old standard, *We'll Meet Again,* as if donning a top hat, tails and a cane, doing a soft shoe toward the heavens. *"We'll meet again, don't know where, don't know when,"* he sings. *"But I know we'll meet again some sunny day."*

It was as if, after all the foreboding songs about the spectre of death, he wanted to say goodbye on a friendly, optimistic note.

As mourners found out at his funeral, that title — *We'll Meet Again* — had a deeper meaning to Cash's life. Inscribed on the back page of the service's program was a poem by Cash titled *Meet Me in Heaven.* The same words were chiseled into the tombstone of Cash's older brother, Jack, who died at age 14 in a workshop accident while he was operating a saw to cut fence posts. His tombstone read: "At the end of our journey, when our last song is sung, will you meet me in heaven someday?"

Cash's funeral on Sept. 15 was a private affair, yet his family and his close friends were so vast that the mourners — most of them dressed in black — lined the street outside the First Baptist Church in Hendersonville. More than 1,500 squeezed into the church sanctuary for the service.

For days, newspapers and TV programs heralded Cash as a one-of-a-kind legend, a great American whose appeal crossed all cultures and levels of society. "No body of work comes close to what his particular body of work is," singer Emmylou Harris told the Nashville newspaper *The Tennessean*.

Cash first came to fame in the 1950s, when he recorded for Sun Records, the small, Memphis-based company also responsible for discovering Elvis Presley, Jerry Lee Lewis, Carl Perkins, Roy Orbison, Charlie Rich and such blues stars as B.B. King, Howlin' Wolf and Ike Turner. Cash was a breed apart, his baritone and foreboding style carried a gravity that other young singers lacked.

His records fused stark, blues-based country and traditional folk with rock swagger. He immediately drew a fervent following with such records as *Cry Cry Cry, Folsom Prison Blues* and *I Walk the Line* — all of them simple, stark recordings packed with meaning.

"He was beyond category," Emmylou Harris once said of Cash. "He was rock 'n' roll, he was folk music, he was country." Or, as his daughter Rosanne Cash said of him, "You can't say Johnny Cash is like anyone else."

Songwriter and actor Kris Kristofferson, a longtime friend, once wrote a song describing Cash as "a walking contradiction." He was a devout Christian who battled drug addiction. He was an anti-war activist who wrote songs honoring the flag and America. He was a social reformer who accepted an invitation to visit President Richard Nixon in the White House, where he was embraced as a true American. And, near the end of his career, he was rejected by the country music community he helped build, only to find a new audience and a revived career by recording stripped-down songs with a rock 'n' roll producer.

His friends included Rev. Billy Graham and Bob Dylan, and his dinner companions might include world leaders like Golda Meir and Al Gore, or rockers like Mick Jagger and Elvis Costello. He could talk to inmates or presidents with the same sense of connection, or discuss religious doctrine or substance abuse with the same sense of authority.

He also inspired a wide variety of artists. He helped several artists get their starts, including the Statler Brothers, Kris Kristofferson, Larry Gatlin, Doug Kershaw, Johnny Rodriguez and Marty Stuart. He influenced country rebels like Merle Haggard, Waylon Jennings and Steve Earle, and artists as important as Bob Dylan, Paul McCartney, Bruce Springsteen and U2 wrote songs expressly for him.

Those kinds of dualities ran throughout his career. No wonder he was the first person to be inducted into both the country music and rock 'n' roll halls of fame. And no wonder Kristofferson wrote of him: *"He's a poet, he's a picker, he's a prophet, he's a pusher, he's a pilgrim and a preacher and a problem when he's stoned. He's a walking contradiction, partly truth and partly fiction, taking every wrong direction on his lonely way back home."*

In all, Cash scored only 14 No. 1 country songs — a measly sum considering his worldwide impact. But some of those songs — *Folsom Prison Blues, I Walk the Line, Ring of Fire, A Boy Named Sue* — rank among the best-known, best-loved American songs of all time. He won 10 Grammy Awards, including the 2002 Best Male Country Vocal Performance for *Give My Love to Rose* from his "The Man Comes Around" album.

But Cash's impact and his connection to fans came because of what he represented to them. He stood for the poor, the disenfranchised, the forgotten and overlooked. He sang for the prisoners and the powers-that-be, for the blessed and for the damned. He sang for all Americans and for everyone who desires a better, more just world.

And there was that voice, deep and ragged, not always on key but always perfect. Surely it's as close to the voice of God as any man has heard. Even when young, his was the voice of experience, the sound of a troubled but proud soul. He sang of love, God and murder, as an album title once correctly put it. But he addressed those topics with a dignity that could conquer all pain and peccadilloes.

3

At **Johnny Cash's funeral,** dignity reigned. More than 40 enormous flower arrangements decorated the chapel. The Fisk Jubilee Singers — a large black choir affiliated with Nashville's Fisk University — opened the service with a hymn. The singer's body lay in an open, all-black casket, photographs of him framed on both sides. Video screens aired filmed highlights of his life.

Rev. Courtney Wilson opened the service with a spiritual sermon and personal reflections on the Cash he knew as a devout parishioner. "Here was a good guy who loved June, loved people and loved God," Wilson said.

Emmylou Harris and Sheryl Crow sang *The Old Rugged Cross* and a Bob Dylan song, *Every Grain of Sand*. Kris Kristofferson, who had his first No. 1 hit as a songwriter when Cash recorded *Sunday Morning Coming Down*, sang an emotion-drenched version of *A Moment of Forever*.

Dressed in a long black coat, Kristofferson also led a prayer. "He was a deeply spiritual man," Kristofferson said of Cash, "a compassionate man willing and able to champion the voiceless and the underdog who was also something of a holy terror: Abraham Lincoln with a wild side. He was a dark, dangerous force of nature that somehow seemed to stand for freedom, justice and mercy for his fellow human beings. He always has, and he always will, all over the world." To end, Kristofferson added, "Johnny represented the best of America and we won't see his likes again."

Franklin Graham, son of the evangelist Rev. Billy Graham, stood in for his father, who was a close friend and traveling companion of the Cashes — Johnny once said he had two best friends, Billy Graham and Waylon Jennings.

The younger Graham presented a fiery religious sermon while praising Cash's willful fight to get past the demons that dogged his life. The preacher also read some messages from his father, who said he'd courted a friendship with Johnny Cash because "then Franklin would look up to me as an important and relevant man." Graham added that his father "looked forward to seeing Johnny and June in heaven one day."

Former Vice President Al Gore told the crowd he was 9 years old when he first met Cash. He commended Cash's prison songs, equating Folsom's cell bars with the prison Cash was in during his years of personal suffering. "Now he is far from Folsom Prison — where he wants to be," Gore said.

Gore also told the assembly that he had spoken with the late singer a few weeks before his death. Cash told Gore he just visited the gravesite of his wife, June Carter Cash, who died following surgery in May.

"He told her, 'I'll be with you soon,'" Gore said. "He told me on the phone that her death was 'the hardest pain I have ever felt.' He was ready."

Gore also commended Cash's direct, honest way of dealing with his problems. Cash, Gore said, wouldn't have sounded right singing a song like Frank Sinatra's *My Way*, with its chorus, "*Regrets, I've had a few, but then again, too few to mention.*"

"No," Gore said, "he had a lot of regrets and he mentioned them all."

His oldest daughter, Rosanne Cash, addressed what she remembered as "two very connected but separate beings. He was the world-famous icon of country music and he was the gentle, conflicted but loving father. I can almost live in a world without 'Johnny Cash,' because he will always be with us," she said. "I cannot, however, begin to imagine a world without Daddy."

Other family members spoke as well, including his stepdaughter Carlene Carter, who jokingly envisioned seeing Cash met in heaven by her mother June, who would be carrying a home-made cheesecake in one hand and a credit card in the other. Reba Hancock, Cash's sister, said: "His rambling days are over, his picking days are done. And I know the Lord will say: 'Well done.' Because Johnny Cash is."

Active pallbearers included Cash's former son-in-law, singer Marty Stuart, singer Larry Gatlin and producer Randy Scruggs, whose famous banjo-playing father, Earl Scruggs, was in attendance. Among the honorary pallbearers were singer/actor Kris Kristofferson, producer Rick Rubin and singers Willie Nelson and Rodney Crowell (another ex-son-in-law of Cash).

Others attending the service were country singers George Jones, the Oak Ridge Boys, the

Statler Brothers, Travis Tritt, Hank Williams Jr. and Billy Walker, and rockers Kid Rock and John Mellencamp.

At the end of the service, the Fisk Jubilee Singers offered another hymn as mourners filed past the casket. Crying echoed through the chapel as the song came to its end.

Marshall Grant, the bass player who was an integral part of Cash's Tennessee Two band in the '50s and '60s, said about his longtime partner that "no one could have held on as long with so much wrong with him."

Grant went on to manage the Statler Brothers and he saw Cash in the best and worst of times. In a *USA Today* interview, Grant said, "John was literally two people. When John was straight, he was the greatest human being that ever walked the face of the earth. However, you give him a couple of minutes behind a closed door, when he walks out, everything turned 180 degrees. He may have had his drug problems, but deep down inside, he was the kindest, most gentle human being that ever lived. You know how they say there will never be another John Wayne, there will never be another Ronald Reagan, there will never be another Elvis Presley. That's all true. There also will never be another Johnny Cash."

In his last months, after the death of his wife, Cash talked of two vultures taking roost on a windowsill outside of his office inside his Hendersonville home. They'd sit and stare at the man inside and Cash stared right back. As his friend Marty Stuart put it, "It takes a guy pretty secure in his position in the world to befriend vultures."

Asked in the last year of his life how he hoped people would remember his music, Cash said, "That it imparted fundamental feelings of love, of life. That it was different. And that it was honest and it had integrity."

And that's exactly how he will be remembered. Or, as rock singer Bono, whose group U2 recorded with Cash in the '80s, said of him: "He was more than wise. In a garden full of weeds — the oak tree."

4

Johnny Cash always spoke admirably of his parents, Ray and Carrie Cash. Admittedly, the Cash family did not have an easy life. Yet Johnny criticized those writers who would over-emphasize the poverty of his childhood, because he didn't want it to reflect on his parents, especially his hard-working father. They never lived on welfare, never relied on handouts. Even when the Great Depression hit, Ray Cash could find work.

The Cashes were of Scottish descent. According to family records, forefather William Cash was a mariner who settled in 1667 in Essex County, Massachusetts. Their ancestry can be traced back to King Duff, Scotland's first king, and Queen Ada. Tellingly, the family coat of arms featured the motto, "Better Times Will Come." The original Scottish name was Caesche, which got shortened and Americanized once the family crossed the Atlantic Ocean.

The Cash descendants landed in Virginia's Westmoreland County in the early 1700s, the same county where George Washington was born. The family resided in that region for more than 100 years, working as planters and fighting in the American Revolution.

In 1810, Moses Cash ventured out from Virginia and settled in Henry County, Georgia. The homestead there was destroyed during the Civil War as part of General Sherman's march through the South and the burning of Atlanta. Johnny's great-grandfather, Reuben Cash, a grandson of Moses Cash, survived the Civil War after fighting for the Southern Confederacy.

Reuben packed his family into an ox-drawn wagon and traveled to Arkansas, where he became a homesteader. Reuben's son, William Henry Cash, was Johnny's grandfather. William Henry grew up in Tupelo, Arkansas, and

became a Baptist preacher, and he and his wife
Rebecca birthed 12 children. The youngest was
Ray Cash.

Ray Cash was 15 years old when his father
William died of Parkinson's disease in 1912. Ray
fought in World War I and he often entertained
his wife Carrie and their seven children — Roy,
Louise, Jack, J.R., Reba, Joanne and Tommy
— with stories of his days as a soldier. He told
of being under the command of the famous
General John J. Pershing and of hunting for
Pancho Villa through Texas and New Mexico.

Ray married the former Carrie Rivers Aug.
18, 1920. He was a good father, full of laughter
and stories and encouragement. He was a good
provider who taught his children the value of
hard work, honesty and religion.

In 1929, when the Depression hit, Ray Cash
continued to work. Cotton was king in that
region, but the market fell out during the hard
years of the early 1930s. Residing in the small
town of Kingsland in Arkansas' Cleveland County,
the elder Cash worked at sawmills and with the
local railroad yards. Sometimes he fed his family
with his .22-caliber rifle, hunting squirrel, rabbit,
opossum and an occasional wild hog or deer.

Johnny was born in the middle of the
Depression — Feb. 26, 1932 — and the hard-
scrabble life of those born to tough times would

always resonate within him. He was given the name J.R. He would change his name to John Ray Cash after he entered the U.S. Air Force.

In 1935, Ray Cash heard that President Franklin D. Roosevelt would open one of his New Deal farming communities in northeast Arkansas near the newly created small town of Dyess, named for W.R. Dyess. He headed the Arkansas branch of a new government agency, the Federal Emergency Relief Administration, which Roosevelt and the U.S. Congress set up to help farmers who had gone bust during the Depression. Ray Cash signed his family up and moved them 250 miles from Kingsland to Dyess into a white, five-room home — the nicest quarters they'd ever had.

Johnny Cash would later describe the Dyess set-up as socialist in nature. The government purchased 14,000 acres of Delta farmland in Mississippi County and created housing and a co-op community for the farmers and their families. The 16 streets that cut through Dyess were all given numbers; the Cash family lived on Road Three. The business district could be found on Road One: a general store, a movie theater, a gas station, a bank, a café, a cannery and a co-op cotton gin. The Church of God could be found on Road 15 in an old schoolhouse.

The Cash clan was fiercely religious, attending

church every Sunday and prayer meetings every Wednesday. Ray Cash taught Sunday school and took on the duties of deacon at the Church of God. Carrie Cash considered herself a member of the Methodist faith and she never transferred her membership to the Dyess Church of God, but she worshipped there faithfully.

The cannery operated like this: The families could bring their self-grown produce to the shop and the cannery would clean, cook and can whatever was handed over. They would hold back one can in five to sell to pay for operating expenses.

The Cash family was given a deed for 20 acres of land with no money down. Their new house came with a barn, smokehouse and chicken coop. Each family got a cow, a mule and an account at the grocery and dry goods store. Everything operated on credit until the first year's crop came in and then the families were expected to start paying for the land and their credit bill.

Cash first experienced the power of music in the Church of God. As an adult, he would remember singing gospel hymns at the church and describe it as the highlight of his week, something he looked forward to during the drudgery of working the fields on weekdays.

Then his father ordered a battery-operated radio from a Sears Roebuck catalog. During the

week, the family would listen to WSM out of
Nashville, WLW out of Cincinnati, WJJD from
Chicago and the powerful border radio station
XERL from Del Rio, Texas. They'd listen to the
Grand Ole Opry on Saturday nights and to
gospel music shows on Sunday.

The Cash children helped pick cotton, back-
breaking work even for a child, and the memory
of it would stay with Johnny all his days. The
children were paid at picking time and because
of that, they all looked forward to participating,
despite how strenuous it was.

J.R. was a strapping young boy with broad
shoulders and by age 8 he joined his older brothers
and sisters hoeing the fields while their father
worked the plow. Carrie Cash would help out,
too, joining the family after she cleaned the dishes
from breakfast and working until it was time for
her to go home and prepare lunch. Then she'd
return, toiling in the fields in the afternoon until
she needed to return home to cook supper. The
younger siblings, Joanne and Tommy, would
pump water and carry it to their family members, just as Johnny had done between the ages
of 5 and 8. The family grew Delta Pine cotton,
with one acre reserved to plant animal feed and
vegetables and fruits for the kitchen table.

As an adult, Johnny would remember his
mother's tears, as she cried in the harsh afternoon

sun, weeping because of the unending harshness of the work in the unbearable heat. He would join his sister Reba in singing hymns to try and pass the time as they worked; J.R. had a knack for remembering the words to songs he heard on the radio and he taught the words to his sister.

His brother Jack, two years his senior, eventually took a newspaper delivery route to help out at home. J.R. worshipped his older brother, who at a young age became a devout Christian and spoke of taking up preaching as an adult. "He became a model — my symbol of goodness and strength," Cash would later write.

On May 12, 1944, when J.R. was 12 and his brother was 14, he tried to talk his brother into skipping his job at a small fence-posting shop to go fishing with him instead. Jack said he didn't feel like working, even telling J.R. and his mother Carrie that he felt like something bad might happen at work. His mother begged him to stay home. But Jack shrugged off his intuition and went to work, because the family could use the three dollars he would earn.

At noon, as J.R. walked back from his fishing pond, he saw his father and the Church of God preacher barreling full-speed down the dirt road. As the car approached the 12-year-old, Cash's father yelled at him to ditch his fishing pole and jump in. It was obvious something was awry. "Jack's been hurt awfully bad," his father told him.

Jack was doing his job at the high school agriculture shop cutting fence posts when he got jerked by an edge of a post and pulled across a table saw. It sliced him from his lower rib cage down through his pelvis, severing his belt in two.

Once they reached home, J.R.'s father took him to the smokehouse and laid out Jack's clothes, government-issue khaki shirt and pants. They were drenched in blood. Ray Cash told J.R. that he didn't think Jack would survive the injury. Then, for the first time in his life, J.R. saw his father cry.

Jack underwent eight hours of surgery, but when it was through, the surgeon told the family that there was no hope, that essential organs were damaged beyond repair. It was only a matter of time. Jack hung on for eight days, several more than the medical experts predicted. But after a week, blood poisoning and gangrene set in. On the last day of Jack's life, J.R. woke to the sound of his father praying out loud. That was another first.

In the hour of his death, with his family gathered around him, Jack spoke of traveling down a river, away from the fire and of hearing the voices of angels. J.R. would later tell the world of his brother's last words: *What a beautiful city!*

*And the angels singing! Oh mama, I wish you
could hear the angels singing!"*

Jack was buried the following day, May 21,
1944. J.R. joined his family in singing the gospel,
bellowing through tears on such songs as *Peace
In the Valley*, *I'll Fly Away* and *How Beautiful
Heaven Must Be*. The next morning, the family
was back out in the cotton fields, hard at work.

Years later, as J.R. "Johnny" Cash struggled
with illness while awaiting his fate, he, too,
would turn to Bible passages and to faith. It's no
wonder so many of his final songs focused on
where he was going, not where he had been.

After Jack's passing, the family struggled on.
Fieldwork remained a permanent part of daily
life, which made the diversions — such as music
— such a pleasure. In the summers, during
lunch breaks, they would gather around the
radio and listen to shows such as *High Noon
Roundup* on the radio station WMPS.

Cash's favorite live performers on the Memphis
station were the duet team, the Louvin Brothers,
who sang simple, stark songs about death,
damnation and deliverance, often leaning hard
on gospel songs during their performances.

In the spring of 1947, he learned that the
Louvins planned to perform at the Dyess High
School auditorium. He was so eager to see them
that he walked to the school two hours early,

getting there in time to see Ira and Charlie Louvin unload their equipment from one of the biggest cars the young boy had ever seen.

Cash would remember the concert as one of the highlights of his youth. He later would eat soda crackers because he saw Charlie Louvin pull some from his pocket for a snack. After the show, Cash stayed until the band left to return to Memphis. As he recalled it, he was the last remaining fan, standing alone under the single light outside the school, watching the car pull away and getting the thrill of his life when Charlie Louvin looked out the back window and waved to him.

Cash became more committed to singing in church after that. His mother encouraged him, accompanying him on the piano. Cash always sang as a tenor, but he struggled to sing on key. As he matured, his voice changed and one day his mother heard him singing around the house in a lower voice. She cried, saying it sounded just like her father's deep singing voice. "God has his hand on you," she told the boy and he began to think that perhaps one day he could sing for people, too, like his heroes on the radio.

Others noticed his talent as well. While attending high school in Blytheville, Arkansas, Cash got a job singing on local radio station KLCN.

5

J.R. Cash was 18 when he joined the U.S. Air Force in July 1950, a week before the Korean War started. He'd left Arkansas once before, moving to Pontiac, Michigan, to work in an auto factory, punching holes in the hoods of Pontiacs at the Fisher Body Plant. He only lasted three weeks before the miserableness of the work and the loneliness of the life sent him hitchhiking home. He briefly went to work in a margarine factory near Dyess, but then decided to enlist.

By now he was a large man, standing 6-feet-1 1/2-inches tall, and he studied radio operation after going through basic training at Lackland Air Force Base in San Antonio, Texas. While there, he met a beautiful, dark-featured young woman, Vivian Liberto, whom he courted.

His skills as a radio operator got Cash stationed in Germany as a cryptographer, where he worked for the Security Service. In Germany, Cash drank beer for the first time, joining with fellow soldiers while on pass, carousing, singing and fishing in nearby lakes. With fellow soldiers he formed a country band, the Landsberg Barbarians, and he began writing songs, setting out the initial versions of such classics as *Folsom Prison Blues* and *Hey Porter*. While leading the Barbarians, he decided to change his name to John Ray Cash.

He encountered a few minor problems in Germany, too. A doctor who'd been drinking operated to remove a cyst from Johnny's face and left a permanent scar; much later, after he was famous, a rumor spread that it had been caused by a knife fight. Also, while out drinking one night, a German girl jammed a pencil in Cash's ear and permanently impaired his hearing. Still, Cash would work his way up the ranks to staff sergeant before getting his honorable discharge July 4, 1954.

During his three years in Germany, Cash and Vivian Liberto carried on a meaningful correspondence. They wrote each other almost daily; Cash would write his letters to her in green ink, something he only used for her. Upon his return, he announced to his family that he planned to marry this dark-haired beauty from San Antonio. Both families protested: Vivian was raised Catholic and their relatives feared the differences in religion would present a problem to the couple.

But Cash made a promise that the couple's children would be raised Catholic and Johnny Cash and Vivian Liberto were married Aug. 7, 1954. Her uncle, Father Vincent Liberto, presided over the vows. Cash was 22 at the time. During all their years of problems, the couple never argued over religion. Cash studied Catholicism and long after the couple's divorce, he would credit his time learning about the Catholic faith as one of the reasons he developed an understanding and tolerance for all different forms of spirituality.

Settling in Memphis, Cash went to work as a door-to-door appliance salesman for a home improvement firm. Elvis Presley was on the radio with his first single, *That's All Right, Mama* and its flipside, *Blue Moon of Kentucky*. Vivian became pregnant with the couple's first child, Rosanne. (They would have three more daughters: Kathleen, Cindy and Tara.) Cash worked hard, but his attention kept returning to music. He enrolled in Keegan's School of Broadcasting, a radio deejay training college.

Meanwhile, his brother Roy introduced Cash to two local mechanics, bassist Marshall Grant and guitarist Luther Perkins. The three of them jammed together almost nightly, with Cash playing guitar, singing favorite country songs and occasionally trying out something he wrote himself. Neighbors and other friends began to gather to watch them and the trio eventually began performing for free on Memphis station WKEM. Right away, they set out to see if they could get a gig playing for money.

Their first show came about from one of their neighbors, who invited the trio to play at his church in North Memphis. Cash and Grant would harmonize on old gospel songs and their repertoire went over well among the Baptist congregation. The trio of musicians decided to coordinate their clothing, but black shirts and trousers were the only things they had in common. So they dressed in black for their church show.

At their performance, Cash introduced his first original tune to an audience. *Belshazzar* was a gospel tune strong with Biblical references and the crowd loved it. From there, the trio began playing nightclubs in western Tennessee and eastern Arkansas. At first, Vivian would travel with Johnny to all the shows, just as Marshall's and Luther's wives did. The families all socialized with each other, too, often dining and hanging out together several nights a week.

Cash took a chance and decided to contact Sun Records on Union Street in Memphis. He telephoned Sam Phillips, the record producer who discovered Elvis Presley. Cash mentioned that he wrote a gospel song that had gone over well with a church audience. Phillips politely rejected Cash's request for an audition.

As Cash wrote in his book *Man in Black*, Phillips told him: "I love those hymns and gospel songs, too, John, but we have to sell records to stay in business. We're a small company and can't afford to speculate on a new artist singing gospel." It wouldn't be the last time the two men had a conversation about gospel music's lack of commercial appeal.

Cash didn't give up easily. He drove down to Sun to try to audition in person for Phillips. But he didn't have an appointment and didn't get past the receptionist. He called again and after getting another rejection, phoned back a week later. Phillips eventually relented and invited Cash down for a tryout.

The audition lasted nearly all day. Cash sang everything he knew — Hank Williams, Jimmie Rodgers, Hank Snow, Ernest Tubb, every country song he'd learned by heart. He eventually got around to presenting his own material, stubbornly starting out with *Belshazzar*, the gospel tune that Phillips repeatedly had turned down. The last song Cash played was *Hey Porter*, a tune he'd written in Germany. Cash didn't feel confident in it, believing it was too simple and unfinished. However, Phillips loved it and put it on tape.

At the end of the day, Phillips gave Cash a recording contract, but with one important stipulation: that the Sun owner could put out the singles he thought would sell best. Phillips also thought the name John R. Cash was too formal. He said they would bill him as Johnny Cash. At age 23, Cash had a recording deal. His life would never be the same.

Cash later would question whether Phillips dealt with him fairly as far as royalties, but he never lost his love or respect for the Sun Records owner, a man Cash would always say had true vision and a real passion for music. "If there hadn't been a Sam Phillips," Johnny would later write, "I might still be working in a cotton field."

Phillips chose a rhythmic heartbreaker, *Cry Cry Cry*, and a train song, *Hey Porter*, as the first Cash single on Sun Records. Cash himself delivered a first pressing to WMPS, the favorite radio station of his youth. The deejay played both sides as Cash stood there beaming.

His first public performance as a Sun Records artist came in Covington, Tennessee, opening a concert for country star Sonny James. Backed by Perkins on electric guitar and Grant on standup bass, Cash strummed his acoustic guitar and sang the two songs from his single. The crowd response was ecstatic and Cash and the Tennessee Two (as he called his band) played the songs three more times in encore after encore. The singer and his bandmates began to realize they were onto something.

The first single sold more than 100,000 copies and rose to No. 15 on the country radio charts. Cash was on his way. Willie Nelson, who saw him in Texas on his first tour, said: "I knew right away that here was a guy who was different. I knew he wasn't gonna be run off too quick."

What was remarkable about Cash's immediate success was that his songs were clearly country. Despite later attempts to label Cash a rock 'n' roller or a rockabilly artist, his stripped-down, simple arrangements, the methodical rhythms and the themes of his music came from country and folk, not from the romping boogie of early rock. From the start of his career to the end, he always called himself a country singer.

But his appeal reached far beyond the country music faithful. As he would write in a song 30 years later, *"I never played much rock 'n' roll, 'cause I got so much country in my soul."*

Shortly afterward, in the summer of 1955, Cash opened a Memphis concert at the Overton Park Shell for label mate Elvis Presley. It marked the first time Cash performed an as-yet-unrecorded song that he called *Folsom Prison Blues*. Again, the crowd reaction was positive.

But it was obvious that on this day, the throngs were eager to move on to the next act. Cash stayed to watch Elvis Presley, whom he'd seen perform a couple of times earlier, at a show in a Memphis drug store parking lot and at an East Memphis ballroom. Each time, Cash would recall, the women screamed and fainted, and the men couldn't take their eyes from the gyrating singer.

6

That same fateful summer of '55, Cash met another singer who would become one of his closest friends. Carl Perkins was, like Presley and Cash, a poor country boy who came knocking on Sam Phillips' door looking for a break. The two met when Perkins was at Sun Studios recording his second single.

Their friendship would also play a role in Perkins' writing his most famous song. Cash loved the rockabilly style which Perkins excelled at and he repeatedly told Carl how good he was at putting a hard rhythm behind a unique blend of country and blues — something they called "bop" at the time, since the term "rockabilly" had yet to be coined.

During one of their musical discussions, Cash told Perkins about one of his Air Force friends, a guy who loved dressing up and lighting up the town. Cash recalled a story where the friend prepared to walk out, dressed to the nines.

"Mighty spiffy," Cash called out. The friend smiled and replied, "Just don't step on my blue suede shoes!"

Perkins immediately responded, grabbing a pencil and writing down the phrase. He told Cash it made a great idea for a song. Cash agreed and said that Perkins would be the best person to write it, since it sounded like a bop tune to him. Perkins wrote *Blue Suede Shoes* on the spot.

Perkins later would repay the debt by making a timely suggestion to Cash. One night on tour, Cash told Perkins he wanted to write a song with substance, something that spoke about being true to yourself and those who love you. Perkins liked the idea and asked Cash what he would call the song. Cash had some ideas — *I'm Still Being True, Because You're Mine* or *I'm Walking the Line* among them. Perkins suggested something snappier, *I Walk the Line*. Cash liked the idea and he would later say that he wrote it as fast as his pencil could get the words on paper.

Shortly after Cash joined Sun, Phillips found yet another raw talent who emerged from one of the poorest backwoods sections of the South. Jerry Lee Lewis first met all of his label mates at once, on a famous day when Presley, Cash and Perkins all happened to be visiting the studio.

Presley was at the piano, singing rock songs like *Blueberry Hill* and gospel tunes that all the men knew. Cash and Perkins were there, too, and started singing with Presley. Then Phillips brought Lewis in to the meet the others and they found Cash and Perkins flanking Presley at the piano, harmonizing on a Southern gospel tune.

Lewis, who grew up singing gospel as well, jumped right in. "Do you know *Will the Circle Be Unbroken?*" he asked. Elvis began playing the tune and the four of them began the famous song. Of course, at the time, Cash had no way of knowing that the song would carry a special significance in his life — it was made famous by the Carter Family, a pioneering country music trio that Johnny would become linked with later in his life.

Lewis eventually replaced Presley at the piano and, as Cash would later write, "He played it like I'd never heard before." The four young men had a blast, carrying on for more than an hour, trading favorite gospel songs and swapping harmonies and leads.

Their joy and camaraderie were obvious, as the world would discover decades later when the session wound up on a recording under the title "The Million Dollar Quartet." It turns out a Sun engineer, Jack Clement, turned on the recording tape while the guys sang and played.

Cash was driving to Shreveport, Louisiana, the first time he heard one of his songs on a car radio. KWKH, the main Shreveport station, played the song. At the time he heard it, Cash was on his way to perform at the *Louisiana Hayride*, the Saturday night live barn dance show sponsored by KWKH. The crowd response was so strong that when Cash came offstage, the *Hayride* management invited the singer to become a permanent cast member of the show. He signed on the spot. It meant he would perform every Saturday night on the show, which was second only to the *Grand Ole Opry* when it came to popular live radio shows in the South.

By the time Cash released *Folsom Prison Blues*, his wife Vivian was pregnant with a second child, Kathleen. While she was happy for her husband's success, the constant touring and traveling created new tensions for the once-happy couple. She worried about their marriage and about Cash's responsibilities as a father. The more he left home, the more forcefully she stated her case — and the more they fought over his role as provider and husband.

But when *Folsom Prison Blues* was released in February 1956, Cash's career skyrocketed. With the song *So Doggone Lonesome* on the flipside, it became a national hit. Both tunes reached into the top five of the country charts.

I Walk the Line, if anything, was even bigger. Cash wrote the song while in Texas on tour as a way of reminding himself to resist the temptations he faced from young, eager women almost every night he performed. He sang part of the song to his friend Carl Perkins, who loved the opening line, "*I keep a close watch on this heart of mine.*" The chorus got right to the point — "*Because you're mine, I walk the line*" — with the simple, beautiful poetry found in the best popular songs.

Released in June 1956, it became Cash's first national No. 1 hit, staying in the top spot for six weeks. Its success led to several important steps in Cash's career. He received an invitation from the *Grand Ole Opry* to join its cast, meaning that the singer had gained country music's most sought-after job — performing on the most successful show in the South.

The hot night in the summer of 1956 when

Cash first visited the *Opry*, he met June Carter. He noticed her sitting backstage, across a room and he boldly walked up to her to introduce himself.

In truth, Cash first fell in love with the beautiful, spirited, big-boned June Carter when on a Dyess High School senior road trip to the *Grand Ole Opry*. June Carter (three years older than Cash) was on the bill. Johnny had heard her on the radio before that and enjoyed what he heard. He especially enjoyed seeing her live, not just because of her beauty — though that certainly added to the pleasure — but because of her engaging comic and musical talents. "She was great, she was gorgeous, she was a star," Cash would write about the moment. "I was smitten — seriously so."

June Carter first heard the name Johnny Cash from her friend Elvis Presley. While touring together the previous year, June heard Elvis singing in a deep, deliberate voice and she didn't recognize the song.

"What's that," she asked him.

"That's Johnny Cash," Elvis said.

"Never heard of him," June replied.

"You will," Elvis elaborated. "He's great and he's going to be famous all over the world."

Elvis was right on both counts. June Carter would come to know Johnny Cash better than anyone else alive. And Johnny's fame would grow to become second only to that of Elvis Presley.

Both Johnny and June felt a lightning bolt the first time they met. As they talked, Johnny made a statement that must've sounded outrageous but turned out to be clairvoyant. Johnny told her directly, "You and I are going to get married someday."

Both of them were spoken for at the moment. Cash was married to Vivian, of course, and June was about to marry Rip Nix, a former football star and boat racer who had become a Nashville policeman.

In his second autobiography, Cash said he made his brash statement because he wanted to plant a seed. "I just wanted to let her know how much I thought of her, how great she was in my eyes," he wrote.

He also started getting booked on national TV for the first time. He appeared on *The Ed Sullivan Show*, *The Jackie Gleason Show*, on Dick Clark's *Bandstand* and on Red Foley's *Ozark Jubilee*. He toured all across America, into Canada and Europe.

His next song, *There You Go*, also went to No. 1 and remained on top for five weeks.

Cash released his first album, "Johnny Cash and His Hot and Blue Guitar," in 1957. The following year, he released the song *Ballad of a*

Teenage Queen, which stayed at No. 1 for 10 weeks and crossed over to reach No. 15 on the pop charts. The song was written by Jack Clement, a Sun engineer and producer who would become a lifelong friend and collaborator with Cash.

Later that year, another Clement song, *Guess Things Happen That Way*, became his fourth No. 1 hit in two years. Also in 1958, Cash recorded *The Ways of a Woman in Love*, which was written by his old childhood hero, Charlie Louvin.

7

Cash was on tour in 1957 the first time he swallowed an amphetamine. It electrified his veins, blew his head off and changed him irrevocably — and he would spend the rest of his life trying to get over the feeling he knew he could get by taking a drug.

He had become friends with fiddler Gordon Terry, who at the time played in Faron Young's band. On a two-car caravan from Miami to

Jacksonville to make the next evening's show, Terry was driving the front car belonging to Young and guitarist Luther Perkins was driving the second. During a pit stop, Terry asked Perkins if he was tired. When Perkins said yes, the fiddler gave him a little white pill with a cross cut into the top. Cash took one as well. The singer later said that he failed to sleep before the next evening's show, so he took another pill from Terry. That night, Cash crackled with energy onstage, even though he hadn't slept in more than a day.

Cash got Terry to give him a handful of the pills. Before long, Cash was buying his own, getting 100 pills for $8 to $10. He discovered other forms of amphetamine, too, which came with such names as Dexedrine, Benzedrine and Dexamyl. Cash got to know all of them very well.

The pills gave him stamina and they were common among entertainers, truck drivers and others who traveled for their jobs. The pills gave him confidence as well, as the preternaturally shy Cash became more animated and energized on stage.

In those days, they weren't illegal, nor were they considered all that dangerous. Most any doctor in any town would prescribe them to a singer. Cash would call doctors in the Yellow Pages, tell them what he needed and he'd get a prescription.

Others noticed, especially friends and

bandmates. Cash became more nervous, more easily agitated. He couldn't keep still. He'd pace the floors at night. He'd get up and take off in a car and cruise the midnight streets. His marriage, already torn by his constant absence, now felt another, deeper wedge being created by amphetamine use. Vivian, from the start, didn't like the pills. She begged him to stop taking them and told him they were going to ruin their marriage and perhaps kill him someday.

Cash also began performing at prisons in 1957, a natural move at a time when one of his most famous songs, *Folsom Prison Blues,* came from the perspective of an inmate locked away for life on a murder charge. His first show came at Texas' Huntsville State Prison in 1957.

"I always felt it was one way of giving back to the American people some of the good they had given us," Cash wrote in *Man in Black.* "By doing a prison concert, we were letting inmates know that somewhere out there in the free world was somebody who cared for them as human beings."

The Huntsville prisoners put on a rodeo once a year, with the endorsement of the warden and the Texas prison system. In 1957, the officials agreed to let them bring in some entertainment as well. They requested Cash — no doubt because of the popularity of *Folsom Prison Blues.*

Unfortunately, a monstrous rainstorm hit just as Cash and the Tennessee Two took the outdoor stage. They tried to gamely press on, but the downpour shorted out Luther Perkins' amplifier and Marshall Grant's wooden bass started to swell and come apart once it was drenched. Cash didn't stop, however, strumming his guitar and singing despite the conditions. The prisoners loved him for it.

Cash's first performance at San Quentin Prison in California took place a few months later, on New Year's Day 1958. Merle Haggard, who would later become a close friend and fellow country music legend, was serving time for armed robbery there.

The San Quentin warden provided entertainment to start every new year. As Haggard later described it, the event was usually a variety show and might include everything from strippers to jugglers to baby pigs to country music singers.

Country music popularity was at a low ebb in 1958, with rock 'n' roll at full strength and capturing the attention of most of America at the time. It wasn't any different inside the prison walls. Before Cash played, Haggard said there were about 15 guys, including himself, who were excited about the young Man in Black, this brashly different kind of country singer, coming to perform in their yard. "Most everybody listened to rock 'n' roll, blues, jazz, whatever," Haggard said.

Cash wasn't at his best that first San Quentin show. Already taking pills and having spent the previous night in San Francisco partying all night, his voice was hoarse and weak for the concert. "When Johnny Cash didn't even show up with a voice, I thought: 'How's he going to pull this off?' " Haggard wondered. "I don't know how he did it, but he did."

He remembers Cash as having a power he'd not seen before in an entertainer. "He could barely whisper his songs, but he was able to capture the imagination of these men who were not necessarily country music fans," Haggard told country star Marty Stuart in an interview in the year 2000. "Even without his voice, he had a leadership ability that was powerful from the moment he took the stage. I don't think there was a guy in the entire joint who didn't like Johnny Cash when that show was over."

Watching Cash also ignited a spark of inspiration in Haggard. "I knew I could do whatever he was doing," he told Stuart. "I knew something like that was within the reach of my limits of talent. I felt like I could do what he was doing and I saw how powerful it was. To tell the truth, it may have been the first ray of daylight I had seen in my entire life."

Even in his dissipated state, or maybe because of it, Cash also touched the crowd with his gospel material. "He brought Jesus Christ into the picture," Haggard said. "He introduced Him in a way that the tough, hardened, hardcore convict wasn't embarrassed to listen to. He didn't point no fingers; he knew just how to do it."

Later in 1958, Cash also made the momentous decision to split with his mentor, Sam Phillips. With his success, Cash felt more desire than ever to record a gospel record. He felt he hadn't truly represented himself to his fans by ignoring a part of his music that was as important to him as the rock and country hits. But Phillips, knowing how hot Cash was as an artist, wanted to keep giving the people what he thought they wanted.

So when Columbia Records came knocking, Cash opened the door. He left tiny Sun Records in Memphis to sign with the internationally established Columbia label. He immediately prepared two albums for release. One was called "The Fabulous Johnny Cash," which included such classics as *Don't Take Your Guns to Town* and *I Still Miss Someone*. The former became his fifth No. 1 hit, staying on the top of the charts for six weeks and selling more than a half-million copies.

The other album, released in 1959, fulfilled

Cash's long-withheld dream to put out an album full of original and classic gospel songs, "Hymns by Johnny Cash." One of the songs was written the week Cash's first Sun single was released. Originally titled *My Prayer* and later changed to *Lead Me, Father*, it remained one of the singer's favorite songs.

His third Columbia album, 1959's "Songs Of Our Soil," accentuated Cash's lifelong obsession with Americana themes. American history, folklore, freedom, farming, Native Americans, trains and the Old West would fill his songs and albums throughout his career. "Songs Of Our Soil" was Cash's first true concept album, where all the material carried a thematic link. He said he was inspired by one of his favorite albums, Merle Travis' "Down Home," which attempted a similar objective of tying songs to an overall theme.

By 1959, Cash moved his family to California. By then, Cindy was born, so his family consisted of Vivian and three young girls. The family rented a house on Coldwater Canyon at first; before long, they moved again, into a sprawling house he bought from another Johnny — *Tonight Show* host Johnny Carson, who was moving to New York to begin his long stint on the famed late-night talk show. Cash paid $165,000 for the Havenhurst Avenue home in Encino; it's worth several million today.

However, the girls reacted badly to the L.A. smog; Rosanne, especially, suffered an allergic reaction to it. So Cash moved farther from downtown L.A., building a beautiful home in the Ojai Valley. He also moved his parents nearby and bought them a home.

But Cash didn't stay there much and the pills began to take a physical toll. A show at Carnegie Hall in New York City was planned for a concert album. But the drying effects of the amphetamines left him too hoarse to sing. Similarly, he disappointed audiences in Las Vegas when his voice was reduced to a dry croak in the desert air.

His first night in jail came in 1959 as well. Drunk and high on pills, he was arrested in Nashville for public drunkenness when police answered a call and found Cash trying to kick down the door of a club that had closed for the night. It wouldn't be the last time that substance abuse would put the star behind bars.

In 1960, Cash created his second consecutive concept album, "Ride This Train." It found the singer tracking through the heartland of America telling stories of coal miners, Western outlaws, lumberjacks and small-town doctors, as well as songs about the dangerous Bayou swamps and the desert's shifting sands. Cash tied it all together with narration that sounded as if it could come from an old schoolroom documentary on American life.

The song cycle and presentation emphasized Cash's desire to have a bigger impact than as a simple singer of earthy, three-minute songs. He wanted his music to evoke the majesty of America and provoke the humanity inherent in the American dream. He hated injustice and poverty, and he wrote and chose songs that tried to touch people's hearts and ignite them to act out against what was wrong in the greatest country in the world.

8

Cash put together an impressive troupe for his 1961 tour. In December 1960, he invited June Carter to tour with him, no doubt encouraged by his obvious attraction to her. Mother Maybelle Carter, June's mother and a former member of the historic country music pioneers the Carter Family, often joined the tour, as would June's sisters Helen and Anita. The Statler Brothers quartet provided gospel-style harmony on the shows as well.

June Carter was a star in her own right by the time Johnny Cash met her in 1956. A vivacious woman, she was both dizzily high-spirited and profoundly down-to-earth. Like Cash, she had a lust for life, but she also grounded herself in old-time religion and considered herself a faithful, dedicated follower of Christianity.

Cash had long admired the Carter Family music, the raw yet pristine mountain sound of A.P. Carter, his wife Sara and her cousin Maybelle, who married A.P.'s brother Ezra. Known as "The First Family of Country Music," and rightly so, the Carter Family was among the popular acts that helped change country music from a largely instrumental genre to one that emphasized vocals.

From 1927 to 1943, they were a solidly popular country music recording and touring act and they rank among the most influential of early American musical stars. They set the mold for country harmony singing and Maybelle, an expert guitarist, created a technique on the acoustic six-string that became known as "the Carter lick," a style learned by nearly every country music guitarist (and many beyond country) to come along in her wake.

Dozens of Carter Family songs rank among the standards of American music, including *Will the Circle Be Unbroken, Keep on the Sunny*

Side,   Wildwood   Flower and *Wabash Cannonball.* As down-home as their sound was, they displayed a wide taste in material, covering ancient folk songs, Tin Pan Alley pop songs, blues songs and plenty of gospel music.

The Carters all grew up in Virginia's Clinch Valley, an area of Appalachia just across the Tennessee border. Their families were farmers and mountain folk, and nearly everyone played an instrument. A.P married Sara Dougherty on June 18, 1915, and the couple regularly performed at churches and neighborhood gatherings.

In 1927, A.P. and Sara auditioned for Brunswick Records and the company offered to develop them into a recording act if A.P. agreed to focus on his fiddle-playing. But he preferred singing and the couple turned down the deal. Shortly afterward, they recruited Sara's cousin Maybelle Addington to join the group on guitar and autoharp.

In late July 1927, the Carter Family trio traveled to Bristol, Tennessee, to audition for Victor Recordings executive Ralph Peer. Their session proved successful and Victor signed them to a recording deal.

When the trio broke up in 1943, Maybelle started performing with her daughters, Helen, June and Anita. The youngest, Anita, actually became the first to regularly perform with the

Carter Family, joining them in 1938 and singing with them daily on a Mexican border radio station, XERA. June and Helen began performing on the radio the following year.

The girls were in their teens when Maybelle took a job with them on a radio station in Richmond, Virginia. Helen played accordion, June told jokes and played autoharp, and Anita (the best singer of the bunch) performed on bass. They continued to sing the old Carter Family songs, as well as covering the popular material of the day. Later they took a more lucrative job at a Knoxville radio station, where, in 1949, they hired young Chet Atkins as their guitarist. They became regular cast members of the *Grand Ole Opry* in 1950.

At the time, country music was rapidly changing. It had become more electric and the dominant styles of the day were a hard-edged honky tonk exemplified by Hank Williams and the smoother, more pop-oriented style of such crooners as Eddy Arnold. Women weren't considered solo artists, though Kitty Wells started to update the role of women in country music with her 1950 No. 1 hit, *It Wasn't God Who Made Honky Tonk Angels*.

However, Mother Maybelle and the Carter Sisters represented a folksier, more old-fashioned form of country music. They were especially popular on the *Grand Ole Opry*, which valued traditional styles, and June's vaudevillian comedy routines also proved to be fan favorites. She developed characters like "Aunt Polly" and "Little Junie Carter," both drawling hillbilly gals who told stories through June's exaggerated, animated characterizations.

The Carter Sisters' style also drew the attention of rock 'n' rollers. Elvis Presley took them on tour in the mid-1950s, sometimes using the whole quartet and sometimes just taking June Carter out as a comedian and singer to warm up crowds for him. Her down-home skits, full of innocent innuendo and cornpone country humor, connected well with Presley's crowd of young females and nervous parents.

Born Valerie June Carter on June 23, 1929, in Maces Springs, Virginia, she learned at an early age to draw on her charisma, her warmth and her wit. Her childhood combined the rugged existence of backwoods Appalachia with the rigors of traveling during the Great Depression with the era's most famous country music group.

Once she started performing with her talented family, June realized she wasn't as gifted vocally as Helen or Anita, so she made up for her limited voice by developing her humor, her dancing ability and her fearlessness into an engaging stage presence.

Once the family moved to Nashville, June developed a close friendship with Hank Williams and his wife Audrey. In a famous incident, a bullet from Williams' pistol, shot in a drunken argument with Audrey, narrowly missed June. Audrey often stayed with June whenever she and Hank fought or separated. "I spent a fair amount of time trying to keep Hank from killing Audrey," June said in a 1999 interview in her Hendersonville home.

She also recalled a turning-point phone call that took place between Hank and Audrey. "I remember him calling out to our house there at the very last," June said. "He told me, 'Look, I'm fixin' to marry. Let me speak to Audrey. I need to talk to her because I'm fixing to do something real crazy. Maybe this will get her straightened out.' When she got to the phone, he told her: 'If you can tell me it's going to be different between us, then I'm not going to marry who I'm fixing to marry.' " The conversation erupted into an argument and within a couple of weeks, Hank Williams married Billie Jean Jones Eshliman. Within three months, he was dead.

In 1952, June married country star Carl Smith, a union that lasted four years and gave them a daughter, Carlene Carter. Meanwhile, in the early '50s, Col. Tom Parker began managing Mother Maybelle and the Carter Sisters, providing them more road work — and that's how they first drew the fortunate spot of being an opening act for another of the Colonel's clients, Elvis Presley. It was Elvis who later asked that June join him on tour as a solo act.

While June and Elvis were on tour, noted movie director Elia Kazan (*On the Waterfront, East of Eden, A Streetcar Named Desire*) asked novelist and screenwriter Budd Schulberg to attend a Presley concert to see if he was a potential movie actor. After seeing a show, Schulberg called back to say he was struck more by the opening act, June Carter. Kazan flew to Nashville to meet her and eventually persuaded her to take an acting workshop in Manhattan.

"I was making money in my own little world and at first I wasn't interested in going to New York City," June said. "But I had left Carl Smith about a year and a half before that because I didn't think he had treated me right. I thought it might be good to get away from Nashville for a while. So I took Carlene and moved up there."

In New York, Kazan introduced her to famed acting teachers Lee Strasberg and Sandy Meisner. She spent two weeks with Strasberg at the Actor's Studio and more than a year with Meisner at his Neighborhood Playhouse. While in New York, she also appeared regularly on popular TV variety shows hosted by Jackie

Gleason and Garry Moore, on the TV soap operas *The Secret Storm* and *The Edge of Night*, and on the Western series *Rawhide*.

Through Kazan, June became close to Marlon Brando, the hottest young actor at the time, and James Dean, who was a fellow acting student. After returning to the road as an opening act for Presley, the future King of Rock 'n' Roll asked her for acting advice. June thought he had the moody charisma of Dean and Brando, and told him so.

"I remember trying to teach him everything I learned in a year and a half — only he had just two weeks," she said. "But he learned quick and I think I really helped him."

She coached him through a short screen test for a serious, dramatic role and she thought it was the best acting she ever saw him do. From there, he went to the set of *Love Me Tender*, the first of his long list of B movies.

"I was never happy with what he settled for," June said. "I decided that if I was going to go into acting, I would not settle. Elvis didn't have to, he just did. I told him, 'If you do this, you could do it right and it would be good. But you be sure and not settle for some crummy thing they give you. You'll be wanting to do just what the Colonel wants you to do and I know what the Colonel is like.' Colonel Parker didn't know what was good and what was bad. He just didn't have a sense for it. He wanted his half and that's what he got."

At the time, June openly encouraged Presley to break his contract with Parker, who got 50 percent of all of Presley's income while cutting side deals where he kept all of the money. "Elvis could have taken him to court," she said. "He should have never paid him that half. 'Don't let him do this to you,' I'd tell him. He would tell me he wasn't going to do it, but he did. I just felt like he settled. I didn't. I moved on and did something else."

After narrowly missing roles in Kazan's critically lauded movies *A Face in the Crowd* and *Wild River*, she starred in another movie, *Country Music Holiday*. When better roles failed to materialize, she went back to Nashville and to touring — refusing the B-movie roles that producers wanted her to take. She later would appear in several movies, including an acclaimed role in *The Apostle* with Robert Duvall, whom she first met when both were New York acting students.

Back in Nashville, she married Rip Nix, a college football star and champion boat racer, and she gave birth to a second daughter, Rosie. She went back to performing on the *Grand Ole Opry*, performing solo and with her mother and sisters.

9

Johnny Cash counted himself among June Carter's fans. He was smitten with her since he first saw her on a high school field trip to the *Grand Ole Opry* and he expressed his admiration for her the first time they met backstage at the Opry. He'd all but proposed to her in that initial meeting, promising they'd someday wed, even though both were committed to others at the time. So when Cash invited June to join his concert tour, it wasn't long before June could feel how strongly their hearts were entwined. But the thought of it shook her, for she could see that this strapping, intense man from Arkansas was battling addiction. "I'd already seen what pills did to Hank Williams," she said, "and I could see them doing the same thing to Johnny Cash."

Still, from the moment she joined the touring troupe, June had Cash's full attention. He requested that she ride in his car between dates. She, in turn, ironed his shirts and stage clothes and made sure he ate well. He made it clear to his bandmates, other performers and crew members that she was off limits to their ideas or advances. She also would be invited on every tour and to every show — from then on.

By 1962, the toll drugs wrought on Cash was becoming more and more obvious to June and others. He no longer scored hits with the same frequency he had in the late 1950s. In 1960, he had only one Top 10 song, the forgettable *Seasons of My Heart*. Nothing in 1961 even reached the Top 10, although he did release a couple of major career songs, the jaunty *Tennessee Flat Top Box*, which his daughter Rosanne Cash would later revive as a hit in 1987, and *The Rebel — Johnny Yuma*, the theme to a hit TV show about a Confederate soldier in the Civil War.

In 1962, he only managed to release two new

singles — mostly because he was missing so many recording sessions. Ironically, the most successful of the singles was a cover of Jimmie Rodgers' *In the Jailhouse Now* and it reached No. 8 on the country charts.

Cash mustered up the energy to complete a 30-hour tour of Korea, playing for the soldiers stationed there. But those who saw the show could see the anxious, twitchy energy, the weight loss and the lack of focus inherent in a man addicted to speed.

That year, Cash planned to record his first live album at New York's prestigious Carnegie Hall. But the performance was such a disaster that the record was scrapped. Cash's voice was shot, a weak, scratchy whisper instead of the usual authoritative, booming baritone. Columbia Records went to great expense to record the performance, but everyone agreed it was a disaster. The tapes were put on a shelf.

The concert was set for May 1962. Cash was a wreck by the time he arrived in New York. He'd been in Canada hunting moose with legendary guitarist and songwriter Merle Travis and fiddler Gordon Terry. Cash had spent the three-day hunting trip on amphetamines, getting little sleep at all. "By the time I got to New York, I was shot: voice gone, nerves gone, judgment gone," Cash wrote. "It was awful, from start to finish."

Still, June found him impossible to resist, and in 1962 she and Merle Kilgore wrote *Ring of Fire*, a song inspired by her conflicted feelings about the Man in Black. "*Love is a burning thing*," the song states in the opening. But the flames can be destructive as well as warming and the song displays June's hesitancy and misgivings.

"*The taste of love is sweet when hearts like ours meet*," the song continues. "*I fell for you like a child, oh but the fire went wild*." By the time the lyrics say that "*it burns, burns, burns, the ring of fire*," you can sense the hellish predicament June felt she faced by falling in love with this troubled star.

"I hadn't told anybody yet, but I was in love with this man," she said later. "I was in love with him, but he was a wild man and there wasn't any indication he wasn't always going to be a wild man."

Cash stayed wild for a while, too. But as their bond grew stronger, June let Johnny know he must quit drugs if she were to fully give her heart to him. "She said she could help me and that she would fight for me with all her might," Cash wrote in *Johnny Cash: The Autobiography*. "She did that by being my companion, friend and lover, and by praying for me, but also by waging total war on my drug habit."

Carter was around Hank Williams and other

entertainers with addiction problems, so she was well-prepared for her new role. She had an understanding into Cash's illness that others might have lacked. She kept talking to Cash about faith, about the difference between walking in the light or in the dark. Rather than criticize or condemn, she appealed to his sense of right and wrong.

"If you always follow your heart, that old heart will get you in trouble," she said. "If you have boundaries that hem and haw and fly up in the air, you might as well give up, 'cause that heart will go boogety, boogety, boogety and you'll get messed up."

Anita Carter recorded *Ring of Fire* first. She put it on an album of folk songs and she cut it with just a guitar and bass, with the tempo much slower than how the song is known today. When Johnny Cash heard her version, he insisted on recording it, too. His version includes bright mariachi horns, a highly unusual move for a country album and something the songwriters didn't consider when creating the song. Cash said the idea came to him in a dream and he ordered the horns the next morning. He got his old Sun Records pal, Jack Clement, to bring horn players from Texas to use on the recording. Clement arranged the session, too, though his participation went uncredited.

When released, a lot of country purists and

deejays balked, saying trumpets didn't belong on a country album. But the fans loved the song. As it turns out, that blast of Mexican-style horns became its most identifiable aspect, and Cash never played a show where *Ring of Fire* wasn't one of his most requested songs.

When Cash released *Ring of Fire* in 1963, his previous single was a somber take on song-writer Harlan Howard's *Busted* that provided a poignant tribute to people who work hard, long hours yet have little to show for it at the end of the day. That song was part of another theme album, "Blood, Sweat and Tears," in the manner of 1959's "Songs of the Soil" and 1960's heavily narrated "Ride This Train."

The central focus of "Blood, Sweat and Tears" was the hammer-carrying folk legend John Henry and, in general, the American working man. Besides *Busted*, it featured a couple of fine Cash performances on *Tell Him I'm Gone* and *Another Man Done Gone*.

But *Ring of Fire* proved to be one of the most successful hits of his career, going on to join *I Walk the Line* and *Folsom Prison Blues* as one of his signature classics. It also became his first No. 1 hit in four years and it got plenty of crossover pop airplay as well, climbing into the Top 20 on the mainstream hit parade.

Ring of Fire also broke Cash out of the

non-commercial box of his Americana theme albums. It revived Johnny's popularity on radio and among fans, reminding them of what a unique force he could be as a vocalist and arranger. His success continued into 1964. He followed *Ring of Fire* with *Matador*, an obvious ploy to continue the Mexican, mariachi-flavored sound of *Ring of Fire*. Though a lesser song, it nonetheless reached No. 2 on the charts. But it never became a permanent part of Cash's stage repertoire, nor would it become a staple on the scores of greatest hits records.

Understand Your Man kicked off 1964 in style. A rocking folk-based tune, it had more in common with Bob Dylan and California country king Buck Owens than it did with Jim Reeves, Sonny James and other artists with hits in Nashville at the time. Nonetheless, it, too, hit No. 1, making it one of the more standout country hits of the era.

Cash, though based in Music City, never experimented with the Nashville Sound, a cosmopolitan sweetening of traditional country that added strings and background choruses in place of fiddles, steel guitars and banjos. It was the prevalent style in country music at the time, but Cash had little to do with it. He always remained an artist in search of his own sound, rather than one who tried to follow what others had success with at the time. In that sense, Cash had more in common with Buck Owens, Roger Miller and other freewheeling individualists who were providing an interesting spark to country music.

Indeed, *Understand Your Man* intimated that Cash was listening to Dylan and other folk and rock artists. The song's arrangement and its propulsive acoustic rhythm tips its hat to Dylan's *Don't Think Twice, It's Alright* in the arrangement and melody.

The flipside of the single also underscored that Cash was looking outside conventional country sources for inspiration. The singer put Merle Travis' standard *Dark as a Dungeon*, a popular tune among young folk artists at the time, as the B-side of *Understand Your Man*. And his no-frills, serious reading of the coal mining song made no concessions to commercial interests.

Cash followed that hit with one of the more socially outspoken songs of his career: *The Ballad of Ira Hayes*, a song written by Native American protest singer Peter LaFarge. The song told the true story of a Native American soldier who, in World War II, became a hero as a U.S. Marine in the battle of Iwo Jima. But when Hayes returned to the country he helped defend, he got treated with racial prejudice. Unable to find good work or respect, he fell into despair and died a homeless alcoholic.

Cash's rendition is brilliantly inspired. He opens with a mournful, solo flute playing *Taps*, then brings in a dark-toned, single-note guitar, W.S. Holland's brushed snare and a choir backing him on the chorus. Cash's recitation is full of passionate, restrained outrage as he tells of this war hero and the treatment at home that led to his drunken death.

"I meant every word, too," he later said of the song. "I was long past the point of pulling my punches."

Cash realized the topic might upset the conservative element in country music and it did. Columbia Records, which rarely intruded on Cash's artistic desires back then, balked when they heard the song, questioning whether the singer was courting controversy. But Cash demanded that his album feature the song — and, to the company's great consternation, he insisted that it be released as a single.

Country radio deejays resisted it at first, saying the material was too dark and upsetting for middle-American airplay. Many stations refused to play it. Cash fired back by writing a letter published as a full-page advertisement in *Billboard* magazine that attacked the deejays. He criticized them for their lack of guts and creative vision and for wanting to "wallow in their meaningless."

At first, the letter only caused the song to get pulled from more stations by program directors offended by Cash's outburst. However, radio listeners liked it and, as the popularity of the song grew, many demanded that their local stations play it. Many did, even some that pledged never to air it. It ended up at No. 3 on the country charts, a remarkable achievement for such a radical song.

Cash learned the song after hearing LaFarge perform it and the two later met in Nashville. Cash pledged to record the song and he more than followed through on his promise. He made the song a centerpiece of his 1964 album, "Bitter Tears," which included five LaFarge songs among its eight cuts. Of all of Cash's Americana theme albums, it's the strongest in both material and performance. It's obvious that Cash, even amid his addiction, still had strong convictions and, as always, those convictions could inspire him to do his best work.

10

Cash's **personal life, though,** was still in shambles and he still ended up in the most insane predicaments, usually brought on by how his mind would misfire when strung out on speed.

In the early '60s, Cash owned a mobile camper that he nicknamed Jesse, after the outlaw Jesse James. He painted the windows black, so he could sleep when he wanted, but also because it fit his mood and style. He'd board the camper and take off from his California home without warning, sometimes in the middle of the night. It was one of many habits that drove his wife Vivian crazy — and left his girls feeling abandoned.

He once flipped the camper on a highway near Santa Maria, California, on a midnight excursion. He accidentally lost control while driving 40 mph and the cabin turned and skidded down the side of an empty two-lane back road. Cash was knocked unconscious and broke his jaw.

Jesse had its comical moments, too, such as the time Luther Perkins drove it into the canopy in the grand driveway in front of the Sahara casino in Las Vegas. Perkins and Cash were talking while Luther drove and the guitarist was so deep in conversation that he didn't notice that the camper was too tall to fit under the front awning. Cash did notice, however, and yelled for Perkins to stop. But the guitarist, unaware of what the problem was, kept going until the vehicle crashed into the canopy, destroying the front entrance to the hotel and casino.

Fortunately, neither Perkins nor Cash were injured. The management of the Sahara replaced the canopy without any complaint and without charging Cash for anything. "They just tore it down, built themselves a new one and never came after us for a nickel," Cash wrote.

However, the most serious incident involving the camper did cost Cash a bundle. He was driving along in the Los Padres National Wildlife Refuge near Ventura, California, when he noticed how squeaky one of Jesse's wheels was. He pulled over to take a look, but by time he got to the wheel, the tall grass it was sitting in caught fire. Apparently, a cracked wheel bearing started spilling oil onto the wheel, which was heated from the friction of driving, the hot pavement and the sun. When the oil hit the grass, it ignited.

With the wind gusting, the fire took off across the grassland before Cash could react. All he could do was watch it consume the side of a mountain as it cut its quick path. Before it was done, the fire had burned the better part of three mountains, all of them part of a wildlife refuge area that was home to the endangered California condors, among other things.

Officials claimed that the fire had decimated the condor population of the area, leaving only nine condors after a previous count of 53. Most had flown off, not died, but the birds no longer inhabited the protected area, where they could be nurtured and kept safe.

By time the fire crews arrived, Cash took his

fishing pole from the camper and headed down to a little creek. He planned to tell authorities he'd been fishing and hadn't noticed the fire until it was too late.

The firefighters arrived, along with planes designed to battle the blaze with chemical repellents from the air. A forestry service official approached Cash and asked if he had started the blaze. The singer said no, but his truck did. The officer took down Cash's contact information and left. Neither he nor the firefighters offered Cash a ride, so he was left in the middle of nowhere with a burned-up camper. He slept on the ground nearby that night.

In court, Cash showed up high on pills and attitude. He smarted off continually to the judge, who let him have it afterward. "Do you feel bad about what you did?" the judge asked him. "Well, I feel pretty good right now," Cash responded. The California forestry service sued him and he ended up paying $125,000 in fines.

By 1965, Cash's habit was more out of control than ever. After a performance at Mississippi State University, Cash returned to his hotel room too wired to sleep, as usual. He tried to douse his energy with whiskey and beer, but he stayed hyped up — and now he was foggy-eyed as well. Well after midnight, long after the small University Motel in Starkville on U.S. 82 closed its shops, he decided to take a walk to look for cigarettes.

Sometime after 2 a.m., a police cruiser pulled alongside Cash as he walked along a residential street, picking flowers and gathering his own drunken bouquet. He told the officers his wife was upset with him, that the flowers were for her.

In his first autobiography, Cash said he was arrested simply for walking down the street and picking flowers. He later wrote a comic song about it called *Starkville City Jail*, making fun of the small-town rubes who would arrest a man simply for being on the street so late at night.

Dr. John Copeland, whose house Cash visited, later told the Associated Press that there was a rumor around town that the singer picked roses meant for the doctor's sister's wedding. "But that wasn't true," Copeland said.

Another rumor had Cash identifying himself from the backseat of a squad car to the arresting officers, one of whom replied, "Yeah, and I'm President Eisenhower."

In truth, there was no Starkville City Jail, as Cash called it in song. He was taken to the Oktibbeha County jail, where the police report says he went into a violent rage when put in a cell. In his book, Cash wrote, "I was screaming, cussing and kicking at the cell door all night long until I finally broke my big toe. At 8 a.m.

the next day they let me out when they knew I was sober."

He left behind his expensive, steel-toed cowboy boots, which were pretty much destroyed from all the kicking. These days, jailers refer to the cell as "the Johnny Cash suite."

He rarely appeared at the *Grand Ole Opry* anymore and he was as likely to cancel a recording date at the last minute as he was to honor a studio appointment. He regularly missed shows, or barely got through them, almost always due to exhaustion or a voice worn so dry and thin that he couldn't sing.

June Carter tried to help. She studied his habits, often sneaking into dressing rooms and hotels to confiscate his pills and flush them or hide them. She persuaded him to accompany her to church on Sunday mornings.

But he always went back to the pills, his worn body feeling the hunger for the energy and false confidence they provided. If June got rid of all his pills, he called hotel doctors or looked one up in the phone book, using his celebrity status to snow them into giving him what he needed.

As the medical profession and police learned of the dangers of amphetamines, they became harder for Cash to secure. He started turning to illegal means. He bought them on the side from druggists or from street dealers. He'd hear of illegal shipments coming in from across the border and would invest in a large cache.

Once, in an addictive fit, he decided to drive to Mexico to score a large quantity of pills. He hired a cab driver in El Paso to drive him to Juarez, Mexico. Cash stayed in the cab as the driver walked into a bar to get his pills. Slumped down in the backseat of a cheap cab on a dirty back street outside a low-down Mexican bar, Cash waited until the driver returned. The driver carried a large bag of what Cash wanted.

Later that day, buzzed on the pills he just purchased, Cash went for a walk in El Paso. He stopped in a pawn shop and bought a 19th-century antique pistol. As he left, a man stopped Cash to tell him he was a fan. They had a conversation about the pistol and the man told Cash he had all his albums.

That night, as Cash sat on an airplane waiting for take-off, he watched as the same man boarded and talked to a flight attendant. They asked Cash if he had a gun on him — it was in a box on his lap — then asked him to get off the plane. Cash did as he was told.

The singer was escorted to an empty room. As he sat down, he saw his guitar and his suitcase — both of which were filled with hidden bags of pills.

After finding his stash — 668 Dexedrine and 475 Equanil pills — the undercover cop who was trailing him and another officer interrogated the singer. They wanted to know where he had hidden the heroin. Cash, flabbergasted, told him he didn't know what they meant.

It turns out the cab driver had bought the pills from a notorious heroin dealer in the bar. So the narcotics agents tailing him thought Cash must've needed to score some heroin. They followed him back from Mexico and on his walk through town that evening.

Cash tried to talk himself out of going to jail, saying the pills were legal and that he could get them from any doctor. But because he purchased them on the black market, he was arrested and booked.

After a desperate night in an El Paso cell, Cash finally got some sleep the next morning, after the pills wore off. He was awakened when the jailer said he had a call. It was Sam Phillips, the Sun Records producer who discovered him. He offered to travel to El Paso or to provide his lawyer. But Cash, embarrassed, turned him down.

The newswires picked up on Cash's arrest. He cried in his cell as he imagined how his parents, siblings and children would react to the news. Others phoned — Columbia producer Don Law, an El Paso deejay — until Cash finally said he didn't want any more calls.

Marshall Grant, Cash's bassist, contacted a lawyer in El Paso and sent him to get his boss out of jail on bail. The next day papers ran a photo of a handcuffed Cash being led from the jail to the courthouse. He was at a new low. It also would be the last night he ever spent in jail.

11

Another infamous moment came when Cash arrived for a guest spot on the *Grand Ole Opry* in 1965. He'd been gulping pills for weeks and showed up as strung out as anyone had ever seen him. His voice was barely a whisper of itself.

As the music started, Cash walked onto the famous Ryman Auditorium stage and tried to take the microphone from the stand. It was stuck. Try as he did, he couldn't pry it free and, wired as he was, his anxiety drove him over the edge.

First he threw down the microphone stand with a loud thud. Then he lifted it, dragged it to the front of the stage and began sliding the weighted iron bottom along the front of the stage, popping each of the electric footlights one by one, until more than 60 were blown. The glass shattered across the stage and into the audience. The band stopped playing. As Cash stalked offstage, an *Opry* executive walked to Cash and quietly let him know that he would no longer be welcome on the historic show.

Angry and humiliated, Cash borrowed June Carter's Cadillac against her wishes and he took it down side streets to avoid attention. He began crying. Rain started to fall and it grew into a thunderous, violent electrical storm. His vision doubly blurred, he nonetheless kept pushing the car ahead, speeding down narrow back streets. At some point, he reached for the windshield wiper controls. But as he did, the car jolted to the side and slammed into a utility pole. Cash broke his jaw and nose and bashed his lips into his upper teeth. He also totaled June's Cadillac in the process. Besides the collision, the tall wooden pole crashed down on the roof and the live electrical wires hit the water puddles and started popping and firing off, lighting up the street like the Fourth of July.

The first police officer on the scene was Rip Nix, June's husband, who recognized what remained of his wife's Cadillac. Cash hid from June for a while, but she quietly let him know that his escapade didn't go over well at home. She also got a new Caddy, paid for by the insurance company.

Cash occasionally tried to quit. He'd go cold turkey. He would rejoin his California place of worship, the Ventura Avenue Community Church, and attend for a few Sundays while staying straight. He made New Year's resolutions and would hold to them for a few weeks at a time.

Amid all this, he released another ambitious story-cycle collection, this one a two-record set titled "Johnny Cash Sings the Ballads of the True West." He didn't just gather cowboy songs and sing them; he presented them as a history lesson, complete with narrative elements, just as he had with "Ride This Train."

The same year, he released one of his best folk-based albums, "Orange Blossom Special." The title song, an old bluegrass standard, would become a part of Cash's show for decades, even after the song became a cliché because of its frequent appearance in the shows of string bands and country stars. The album itself features three songs by Bob Dylan — *It Ain't Me, Babe, Don't Think Twice* and *Mama, You Been On My Mind.* It also includes Cash's classic version of *Long Black Veil,* a song written by Nashville stalwarts Marijohn Wilkin and Danny Dill.

Still, his albums continued to sell. His "Ring of Fire" album, released two years earlier, was given a gold record for selling more than 500,000 copies. Cash also appeared in a movie, *Hootenanny Hoot,* in 1965.

But the demons returned and his addiction flared with a vengeance. Cash took to daredevil acts that seemed to taunt death. He steered his Jeep off of a California hillside and let it crash down the rocks and brush, seeing where and how it would land, his knuckles squeezed white on the wheel.

He began leaving home to drive into the California desert, deep into Death Valley, an allegory for his condition if there ever was one. He walked alone deep into the stark, dry, deserted land, often carrying a gun and the Jeep stocked with beer.

One night in the Mojave Desert he crashed his Jeep right through a U.S. Naval Grounds gate that read, "No Trespassing." He found a paved road and noticed huge pockmarks in the soil and some burned-out vehicles. He realized he'd driven onto a bombing range. A Navy vehicle eventually caught up with him, telling him the area was full of land mines and unexploded bombs. He wasn't arrested, just told not to return.

Eventually, life at home in California grew so tense and explosive that Cash began staying in Nashville, away from his family. Vivian filed for divorce. The couple had four girls by now, with Tara the latest arrival.

Cash planned to fly to Los Angeles for Christmas in 1966, but he got off the plane at every stop. He visited nightclubs, drinking and partying with whoever would recognize him. He finally arrived late on Christmas Eve, after everyone gave up on his promise to visit. Cash would describe it as a joyless holiday. He felt estranged from his children and his marriage had clearly ended, even if the divorce wouldn't be final for a few months. He left the day after Christmas.

At the invitation of Mother Maybelle Carter and her husband Ezra, Cash would sometimes stay at the couple's home in Madison, Tennessee. They knew of his troubles and they hoped their generosity would keep Cash from seeking pills on downtown Nashville streets.

"My parents were happy, after they got to know them a little, that I was spending a lot of time with the Carters, because they were people who truly cared for me, as did June," Cash would say later in life. "So it was their love and care for me, and the musical influence and the musical sharing, that was very binding. And we're all still kind of bound up that way."

Cash constantly lost his key to their house and if he arrived late at night, he kicked the door until he got through. After splintering every door and breaking a few windows, he moved out, renting an apartment not far away in Madison.

Soon afterward, Cash ran into a newly arrived country singer, Waylon Jennings, while out on the town. Big and strapping like Cash and with a similar mix of macho swagger and brooding sensitivity, the two recognized each other as kin. When Cash learned Jennings needed a place to live, he invited the newcomer to share his Madison apartment.

Neither man stayed home much. Jennings, in his way, was just as wild as Cash. Eventually, Waylon asked his new friend why he stayed in a small apartment when he could afford a mansion. Cash said he'd feel guilty paying for two homes when his girls all lived in California. Jennings' reply stuck in Cash's mind: He said that maybe if he bought a nice house, the girls would visit.

Cash took the advice to heart. He went for a drive one day, drawn to the rolling hills and gentle farmland of Hendersonville. He knew several celebrities — Roy Acuff, Lester Flatt,

Red Foley, his friend Roy Orbison — all lived in the area. During one drive, he noticed an unusual structure being built right at the edge of Old Hickory Lake.

At one end, the house had two large, circular 35-foot rooms. At the bottom, a 130-foot room extended outward, featuring a large kitchen and bath. It was built out of 100-year-old timbers gathered by its builder, Braxton Dixon. Planned as a Dixon family home, when Cash first approached him to ask a price, Dixon said it wasn't for sale. But Cash persisted and eventually named the right price.

12

In the fall of 1967, Cash weighed 161 pounds. He was about 40 pounds underweight for a strapping, broad-shouldered man who stood nearly 6-feet-2. His thinness had nothing to do with food, of course. The pills, especially the amphetamines, were wearing down his flesh.

"I was in and out of jails, hospitals, car wrecks," he wrote about himself. "I was a walking vision of death and that's exactly how I felt. I was scraping the filthy bottom of the barrel of life."

It showed on stage. He slurred his words or forgot entire lines and looked to his band for help. Sweat drenched his stage clothes and his face was locked into an anxious scowl. He wouldn't talk to crowds between songs, just let out a hoarse cough — his throat raw and parched — and try to remember the opening lines of the next tune. He looked at his watch instead of into the eyes of his crowd. He cared more about how much longer he had to stay on stage than he did about the reaction of those who had paid money to see him.

When the show ended, he immediately rushed to his dressing room for another handful of pills. Sometimes the frustration would grow too intense and he'd smash furniture, break mirrors, punch his fist through a door or wall, smash another guitar into splinters. He destroyed hotel rooms long before rockers made it fashionable. The rockers saw it as an extension of their rebellion and youthful exuberance. But Cash wrecked rooms purely out of rage, he said.

As the pills took their hold and started causing his muscles to spasm, he started to drink —heavily — and pace. He'd walk the floors of the dressing rooms, pace hotel rooms and floors or hit the streets after midnight and walk alone down darkened city streets. If he had downers, or barbiturates, he gulped a handful of those to try and knock himself out so he could sleep, however fitfully. Then he repeated the routine the following day. And the one after that.

Should his pill supply dwindle, he took desperate measures to make sure it was replenished. He had contacts and dealers stretched across the country. But that wasn't always enough. A couple of times in the '60s, he began to plot how he could burglarize a pharmacy. Paranoia ripped his mind as well. He carried a gun and accused others of plotting against him.

June regularly voiced her fears. But Cash ignored them; often stomping from a room as soon as the topic of his addiction was raised. Sometimes he said he would change; sometimes he told them to mind their own business, he was fine — even though everyone knew better. His loved ones no longer just worried that he might die; it came to a point where it seemed inevitable.

Indeed, once, he almost purposely took his life. Feeling so low that he couldn't see an end to the bottom, he prepared himself for suicide in October 1967. He planned to travel to Nickajack Cave on the Tennessee River, just north of Chattanooga. It led into an enormous system of caves that went all the way into Alabama. Cash planned to walk as deep as he could into the caves, so deep that he'd never find his way out. He wanted to be found that way — if he was found at all.

He got as far as crawling into the cave. He kept going until his flashlight's batteries wore out, some two or three hours after he began. He can remember lying down in total darkness.

But lying there, he felt the hand of God. Something, some unknown and unrequested force, sobered his mind and powered his body. It wasn't his time, Cash realized. He began to crawl, unable to see anything, not knowing where he was going. He followed where his instincts told him to go. He got to where he could see daylight and he followed it. When he reached the end of the cave and stepped out, June stood there with a basket of food and drink. His parents were there, too.

Having hit bottom, John told June and his parents that he wanted help. June contacted a psychiatrist, Dr. Nat Winston, but before the doctor arrived Cash broke down, found some pills in his house and swallowed them. Alone, he took his tractor for a ride near the lake. At some point, riding near the cliffs, the ground gave way and the tractor toppled toward the water. It turned over, barely missing Cash's body. He crawled from the wreckage to find Dr. Winston, June Carter and the homebuilder, Braxton Dixon, running to help him.

The doctor suggested that someone stay with him full-time. June talked it over with her father Ezra, who recommended she move in with Cash to help save his life. They cut him off from all friends. He went through withdrawal symptoms, battling nightmares and tearing up rooms looking for more pills. June prayed for him and she encouraged Cash to pray, too.

He made it. Three weeks of sobriety and Cash awoke a healthier, freer man. Later, he would say that June didn't save his life. No one can do that for an addict; he had to do it for himself. What she did, he said, was "lift me up when I was weak, encourage me when I was discouraged and love me when I felt alone and unlovable. She's the greatest woman I have ever known. She's got standards. She's got tradition. She's got dignity."

For his first trip out of the house, he went to the First Baptist Church of Hendersonville with June on a Sunday morning. That evening, Cash performed his first show in more than a month, a benefit for Hendersonville High School. He closed with a gospel song.

As Cash eased back into life on the road, where his addiction would face its biggest tests, he flanked himself with friends. June Carter always went with him, keeping a watchful eye while their love for each other grew stronger.

Carl Perkins was another friend Cash recruited

to join his band. But when Cash kicked his pill habit, it forced Perkins to confront his own problem with alcohol. He would drink a fifth of bourbon every day, even before going on stage. Perkins played the Hendersonville show, as did the rest of the band, all of them cautious yet hopeful about Cash's recovery. But two weeks later, when another full Cash tour began in San Diego, California, Perkins arrived drunk for the concert.

Again, it was June Carter who gave him a heart-to-heart talk, speaking of God's love and ability to help the sick heal themselves. Perkins cried, saying he was beyond help, that God wouldn't save a wretch like himself. Carter mentioned how sick Cash had been only a few weeks earlier. She encouraged Perkins to look at his old friend, to see how his life had turned around, how he was revitalized with the help of his faith.

Later, Cash re-boarded the bus to talk to Perkins, who was in the back alone nursing a hangover. As Cash walked in, Perkins was coming down the aisle, holding a bottle of whiskey in his fingers. Cash asked Perkins if he planned to drink it. He answered no, he planned to throw it in the ocean. Cash backed up, letting him by. With Carter, Cash and the entire band and crew watching, Perkins staggered through the sand and, with all the might he could muster, hurled the bottle into the Pacific waves. Perkins then dropped to his knees and everyone could hear him asking for God's mercy.

Perkins retired to the bus and slept for hours. He looked refreshed upon waking and a smile returned to his face. "I'm going to live," he gently told Cash that day. Perkins never took another drink for the rest of his life.

The following year Perkins wrote what ranked as his most famous song after *Blue Suede Shoes*. Cash was the first to record the song, *Daddy Sang Bass*, and his version remains the most famous, though it's been recorded by thousands of gospel, country and bluegrass bands since Perkins wrote it in 1967.

The newly happy couple celebrated their relationship with their first duet album, "Carryin' On with Johnny Cash & June Carter." On the cover, Cash still looks frighteningly gaunt — but he was gaining his strength and his weight back slowly. Carl Perkins wrote the liner notes and most of it is humorous, with Perkins starting out: "Twelve long miserable years have passed since I was introduced to Johnny Cash." But, amid the humor, he underlined the transformation he saw in his friend Johnny Cash since June dedicated herself to making him a better man.

"June is affectionately known as 'Brindl' and poor little Brindl has had a tough time these last few years," Perkins wrote. "She has fought a battle to tame a man with a wild streak — trying and succeeding most times in eliminating the streak. She has terrible tactics for doing this, such as cooking ham on a shaky stove while enroute to High Point, North Carolina, in a beat-up Dodge motor home, pressing suits, haircuts, hot biscuits and all."

In some ways, the couple's music accentuated how different they were at their cores. June was naturally effervescent, a bubbly, talkative, personable woman with a bright, upbeat personality. Johnny was dark, somber and broodingly quiet by nature, not prone to making friends easily and he rarely talked without first giving his words plenty of thought. But that's where the balance came in. June gave Cash a playful sense of life; Cash, in return, anchored June with a weight that grounded her in reality.

The two first recorded together in 1965 when they put out their duet version of Bob Dylan's *It Ain't Me, Babe*. (Decades later, June said she couldn't hear the words to that song without thinking of Dylan's lovely ex-wife, Sara, the mother of the singer's children.) Set to a harmonica and a steady acoustic-driven beat and with horns goosing the arrangement with high-impact blare, Cash offers the same warning Dylan wrote for his wife Sara: *"You say you're looking for someone who's never weak but always strong, to protect and defend you, whether you are right or wrong. Someone to open each and every door, but it ain't me, babe, it ain't me you're looking for, babe."*

The song climbed to No. 4 on the country charts — remarkable considering who wrote the song and what it said amid the conservative country music climate of the mid-'60s.

The next song did even better — and it went on to remain the most famous duet by this most famous couple. *Jackson*, about a couple that *"got married in a fever"* only to see the fire burn out, showed off June at her most feisty and she inspired Johnny to be as animated and playful as he'd ever been. Yet another Top 10 single followed with *Long-Legged Guitar Pickin' Man*, another he-said, she-said song.

On stage, it began to show how comfortable they were with each other as well. The spark, the fire and the camaraderie now flared for everyone to see. Cash was happy in public for the first time since the '50s and smiled and joked with crowds openly. June couldn't have contained her natural humor if she wanted to — it bubbled over regularly. To anyone who saw them, they were obviously two people in love.

Carter was born into country music royalty. She achieved great success on her own in music,

TV and movies. But her greatest legacy came on two levels. On the most obvious level, she became a partner and soul mate to one of the most influential and impactful American singers of all time and she helped save him from himself and nurtured his health, his confidence and his joy. On another level, the one known to the thousands of people she touched in her life, she motivated the famous, the infamous and the unknown with her unconditional love, high spirits and gracious living.

13

Johnny Cash began performing in prisons early in his career, appearing at the Huntsville State Prison in Texas in 1957. Folsom State Prison in Represa, California, seemed a natural venue for Cash to perform. After all, his most famous song was about being locked up for life in Folsom Prison. Cash first played there in 1966, at the request of his family's California preacher. The response was explosive and as

soon as the show was over, Cash started dis-
cussing the idea of making a live album at a
prison someday.

Robert Johnston, a producer with Columbia
Records, got excited about the idea. He set
about making arrangements with the California
penal system. On Feb. 10, 1968, Cash and his
band arrived at Folsom Prison, outside of the
state capital of Sacramento, ready to make a
record.

Folsom Prison is a maximum security prison
that also holds some minimum security
inmates. Opened in 1880 on 40 acres, it's
California's second-oldest state prison and has
five general population cellblocks.

Cash brought his entire musical entourage. He
had his band, bassist Marshall Grant, guitarist
Luther Perkins and drummer W.S. Holland. Carl
Perkins (no relation to Luther) was with them as
well. June Carter and the Statler Brothers filled
out the program.

Before he went to sleep the night before the
show, Cash's preacher knocked on his door. He had
a tape of a song by a prison inmate he wanted Cash
to hear. The singer was reluctant; he needed some
rest and he had listened to thousands of tapes
from strangers in his day. But the preacher insisted
and Cash didn't want to disappoint someone who
was so important to him.

He played the song *Greystone Chapel* by an inmate named Glen Sherley. Cash was touched. It was about the prison church and the role it played in inmates' lives. Cash listened to it repeatedly until he could sing along with the tape.

The audience was asked not to applaud when Cash first appeared. For the sake of the recording, the crowd was to wait until the singer said his trademark, "Hello, I'm Johnny Cash." They did, with only murmurs and a few yelps breaking the silence as Cash walked onstage. When he stated his greeting, however, the place detonated with cheers.

From the outset, Cash was in control. Healthy again, his voice was robust and packed with passion and authority. His version of *Folsom Prison Blues* owned a new swagger and snarl. Smartly, he followed it with a Harlan Howard song, *Busted*, about a man struggling to make ends meet and the embarrassment of what it's like not to be able to pay bills or properly clothe your kids. It reached beyond the criminal element and related with the idea of poverty, something many of the inmates no doubt knew all about.

It was like that throughout the show. Cash perfectly organized his show's set list, altering his normal show to choose material that would carry an emotional impact with an audience of prisoners.

There's Merle Travis' *Dark as a Dungeon*, a coal-mining song that just as easily could be about life in a penitentiary. There's *I Still Miss Someone*, a lonely love song about not being able to see the one who owns your heart. There's *25 Minutes to Go*, a novelty song about counting down the time waiting to be hanged at the gallows. There's *Long Black Veil*, about a man who took a murder rap rather than use his alibi, which was that he was in bed with his best friend's wife. There's *The Wall*, a dramatic folk narrative about a prisoner planning his escape — or was it, as the song asks in the end, a man knowingly setting up his suicide by a guard's rifle? There's *I Got Stripes*, about the daily life of a jailbird. And there's *Green Green Grass of Home*, about a prisoner dreaming of going back to the family homestead, only to realize when he wakes that it's his execution day.

And there's the song Cash would've never sung to his church-going audience. *Cocaine Blues* is a ribald old blues song about a drug addict who kills his cheating lover and goes on the run before getting 99 years in the pen. The song ends with the singer in prison, serving his time and shouting: "*I can't forget the day I shot that bad bitch down.*" Then, as a final warning, he takes on the exaggerated voice and shouts: "*Come all you guys and listen to me, lay off that whiskey and let that cocaine be!*" The crowd erupts with lusty screams, as if ready for a jailbreak.

He also talked their language. In the extended, full-concert version of the album that was released in 1999, Cash adopts the rough language of his audience in order to pull them further to his side. "I want to tell you that this show is being recorded for an album release on Columbia Records," Cash told them at one point. "And you can't say hell or s**t or anything like that."

Cash knew Glen Sherley, the inmate who recorded the tape he heard the previous night, was sitting in the front row. The singer saw him clapping and singing along. As the event progressed and each song receiving thunderous applause, Cash eventually announced it was time to go, but he wanted to do one more song.

"This next song was written by a man right here in Folsom Prison," Cash told the crowd. "Last night was the first time I ever sung this song. It was written by our friend Glen Sherley. We hope we do your song justice, Glen. We're going to do our best."

Glen Sherley was shocked, understandably. No one tipped him off to Cash's surprise. As Cash described it, Sherley's face turned red, then ashen pale. By song's end, tears were rolling off his cheeks.

In the liner notes to "Johnny Cash at Folsom Prison," the singer relates the emptiness and hopelessness that besets many prisoners. He also commented on why he performed more than 30 concerts inside prison walls. "Prisoners are the greatest audience that an entertainer can perform for," Cash wrote. "We bring them a ray of sunshine in their dungeon and they're not ashamed to respond and show their appreciation."

The album went on to become an American classic and one of the most vibrant testaments to Cash's power as a performer. It sold more than 6 million copies, hooking many listeners who thought they'd never listen to or buy a country music album. At a time when rock and soul ruled the airwaves, Johnny Cash made country music vital and respectable again.

In the liner notes to the 1999 reissue of the record, country rocker Steve Earle wrote, " 'Johnny Cash at Folsom Prison' was the first 'country' record I ever listened to from beginning to end." He explained that Cash struck him as being different from the other country singers he'd ignored. "Cash was a BADASS. He wore a lot of black and he sang about murder and dope and adultery and ghosts. He had genuine attitude. His music, more than anyone else's, was simultaneously country and rock."

By the end of 1968, Johnny Cash seemed to genuinely settle into a life with more peace and balance. Others began to realize the change, too. His ex-wife Vivian allowed the girls —

Rosanne, Kathy, Cindy and Tara — to visit the new Cash home in Hendersonville. Rosanne was 13; Kathy was 12; Cindy, 9, and Tara, 6. June lived nearby in Madison with daughters of similar ages. Carlene, the oldest, was 12. Rosie was 9. The girls mingled well and the families began spending more time together, usually at the Hendersonville home.

Johnny and June became nearly inseparable. They toured together and spent most of their time off the road together, as well. They'd been close for years, but Cash's sobriety brought a new level of intimacy to their relationship. Now they actually relaxed together, finding ways to be together in silence as well as in activity.

Considering all the quiet and private times they spent together, Cash picked an unusual moment to propose. His question was conventional. "June, will you marry me?" he asked. Only there were 5,000 people in the audience in London, Ontario, and Cash asked the question into the microphone in the middle of a show. At first, June just stared, unable to respond. Cash asked the question again, also saying that he loved her. June was too shocked to answer, only muttering: "Let's go on with the show."

The audience would have none of that. They shouted choruses of "Yes! Say yes!" Cash smiled in a way that said he would not let her off the hook.

He told her they wouldn't continue until she answered. Her lips parted into a slight smile as well. "All right," she responded. "Yes. Yes, I will."

Cash leaned over and kissed her while the crowd cheered. He told her he couldn't wait any longer; that at that moment he knew it was time to ask. They then sang *If I Were a Carpenter*, a song that was a top hit for them as a duo: *"If I were a carpenter, and you were my lady, would you marry me anyway, would you have my baby?"*

It had been three months since Johnny Cash took an amphetamine pill. He felt like a new man and he was ready for the next stage of his life to commence with the woman he loved.

At home, Cash found a new way to occupy himself: He began reading with a vengeance. He devoured history books and anything about religion, poring through novels like *The Silver Chalice* and *The Robe* while studying Christian and Jewish history as well. Cash and June traveled to Israel for the first of many times in early 1968.

While staying at the King David Hotel in Jerusalem, June woke up one morning and told Cash she had a dream about him. "I saw you on a mountaintop in Israel and you had a book in your hand — maybe it was a Bible — and you were talking to millions of people about Jesus."

June's words shook Cash. As connected as he was to his faith and as open as he was about singing gospel songs and speaking out in concerts about his religion, he didn't feel comfortable thinking of himself in the kind of role June described. But after he talked to June more, he thought maybe the answer was that he was to make an album or head a project that took the word of Christ to the public. Two days later, while visiting the Sea of Galilee, June tugged Cash's shirt sleeve, pointed toward the distance and said, "There's the mountain I dreamed about where you were standing."

Shortly after their return, they received horrible news. Luther Perkins, whose guitar playing was integral to Cash's sound, died from burns received in a house fire. Johnny came to believe that Luther likely fell asleep on the couch, a cigarette burning in his fingers. He didn't die immediately; but after being taken to an intensive care burn unit, Johnny, June, Luther's wife Margie and everyone else knew it was inevitable. It reminded Johnny of standing at the death bed of his brother Jack, knowing there was nothing he could do but watch and pray as someone he loved dearly passed slowly from this world.

For a while, Carl Perkins filled in as lead guitarist. Then one night, Perkins and Marshall Grant didn't make a show on time because of a canceled flight. Cash thought he was going to have to perform with just W.S. Holland on drums and June on vocals. But just before the show, a short, bold young man stepped forward. Bob Wootton introduced himself, said he was a guitarist and that he knew all of Cash's songs. Desperate, Cash agreed. Wootton indeed proved he knew every song, playing them note perfect to the recordings, even getting the keys right for every song without prompting from Cash.

Afterward, Wootton didn't hesitate to ask for the job that was unfilled since Luther's death. Cash was reluctant; he only had one lead guitarist for the 13 years of his career. Cash talked it over with Holland and his wife, and they both decided he was quite good. The timing seemed fateful.

They decided to put him on stage with the rest of the band and see how it worked. The first show went great, it was almost impossible to believe that Wootton was walking into a situation where everyone else had been together for so long. But they all agreed they sounded good together. Wootton would fulfill the lead guitarist role for the rest of Cash's life.

Johnny and June married March 1, 1968, at a church in Franklin, Kentucky. Merle Kilgore, who wrote *Ring of Fire* with June Carter and was one of Johnny's closest friends, served as best man. Hundreds of guests attended the service and the lakefront party afterward. No liquor was served. The golden rings they exchanged were purchased in Jerusalem and inscribed, "Me to my love and my love to me." June Carter Cash moved her children, Carlene and Rosie, into the Hendersonville home. Cash welcomed them and as often as he could, he brought his girls from California to visit and stay.

Before the end of the year, Cash decided to return to Israel to record an album, "Johnny Cash in the Holy Land." Once it was released, June took a look at the album cover and said, "That wasn't my dream." Perhaps there was more in the future for Cash and his religious work.

14

Cash and his wife agreed to perform for the troops in Vietnam in January 1969 and it led to the singer's first slip in his recovery. He caught a fever while traveling in the Philippines, one of the stops along the way. When a doctor visited and recommended rest, Cash told him he had two shows the next day for soldiers and he hated to miss them. He asked the doctor, who had no idea of Cash's troubles, if he had any

Dexedrine or something that would get him through the show. The doctor offered a dozen Dexamyl and one was meant to last 12 hours.

Cash took two pills before dinner, then two more in the morning after a sleepless night. By show time, Cash had taken more than six more pills and his wife knew he was high. She protested when he requested a double shot of brandy, but he told her to mind her own business — just like in the old days.

Cash made it through the show, barely. He was hoarse, just like before. By the time they reached Vietnam, he had pneumonia. Yet, for days, as he toured Southeast Asia, he kept gulping more amphetamines, always able to convince another doctor he needed them.

Finally, bottoming out in front of 2,000 servicemen, Cash performed his songs in a croaky whisper and then apologized. He went back to his hotel, confessed to June that he took six or eight pills that day and the two kneeled to pray for forgiveness and strength. The next day, Cash flushed his remaining pills while June watched. As Cash later put it, "I lost a round in the middle of a long winning streak."

With the Folsom Prison live album setting sales records, Columbia Records encouraged Cash to make another prison concert album. He often visited San Quentin State Prison, located a little north of San Francisco. He once entertained a young Merle Haggard there while Haggard was serving time for attempted robbery. So Cash suggested the show take place there.

Cash was known for supporting bright new songwriters, especially those who took chances and broke rules. The day before he left to record the San Quentin album, he got a call from a friend, a Nashville music publisher. He wanted Cash to hear a song by Shel Silverstein, a writer he knew Cash liked. Cash asked the name of the song. *A Boy Named Sue*, he was told. Cash laughed. That didn't sound anything like a song he would record. He didn't like cute, novelty songs.

Yet his curiosity was provoked. Silverstein was an interesting guy, someone Cash found clever and funny. He wanted to at least hear the song he planned to turn down.

Cash listened to the demo tape of the record. He had to admit, he liked it. It made him laugh, yet it had a certain drama and a moral lesson to it that he enjoyed. He agreed to take the tape and to consider recording it sometime.

The morning he was to leave for San Quentin, June stopped him as they were walking out the door. "Did you remember the tape of that new song?" she asked. Cash hadn't. He went back and picked it up, tossing it and the lyrics into his bag.

The San Quentin concert took place Feb. 24, 1969 — exactly one year and two weeks after the Folsom Prison concert and two days before Cash's 37th birthday. It was Cash's fourth appearance at the infamous California prison, the first one had been Jan. 1, 1958 — the time Merle Haggard saw Cash perform and felt further pushed to pursue a music career of his own.

Opened in 1852 and covering an enormous 432 acres, San Quentin is California's oldest penitentiary and it's where the state's death row inmates are housed. It holds the state's only gas chamber. The Cash entourage noticed a different level of tension at San Quentin than at Folsom.

"We had come to see the lost and lonely ones," June Carter later would write about her visit to San Quentin with her husband. "I married this man, Johnny Cash, and there was something in him that drew him to these men. He had been in their shoes, at least some of them. He had hollered louder than any of them, when he was picked up and jailed for disturbing the peace, not just once but seven times. All of that was a long time before we were married and this was a day not like any other will be again."

This time, Bob Wootton performed in place of the late Luther Perkins. The entire Carter Family vocal group — June, her mother Maybelle and sisters Helen and Anita — joined the Statler Brothers, Carl Perkins, bassist Marshall Grant and drummer W.S. Holland. Besides the Columbia Records engineering crew, a Granada TV crew from England had received permission to film the event.

While walking in front of the cells prior to the concert, June Carter said she felt fear. "San Quentin is a maximum security prison," she wrote in the liner notes to the live CD. "Some men are here for armed robbery, rape, pedophilia, arson, murder. And there were a few innocent men. It felt like a dream."

A guard cautioned the Cashes not to look the men in the eye, but to gaze above them at the walls. "I'd never felt such a burden on my husband's heart and I'd certainly never felt such a burden on mine," she would later say about entering San Quentin. "I held tighter to his hand and I was still afraid. I remember praying, 'Lord, God, help us all and show us the way.' "

The men called out to them as they passed through the prison ranks. "What is John really like, June?" an inmate on death row called out. She answered, "He's tall, he's lean and he's mean. There's just not another one like him."

Another prisoner asked Cash what he thought of San Quentin. Walking with the warden and other prison officials, Cash didn't answer, but he leaned over to June and whispered, "San

Quentin is a hell hole. It ought to rot and burn
in hell for all the good it does."

June, in her Christian way, shared her husband's feelings about prisons. As presently set
up, they didn't do as good a job of rehabilitating
criminals as she thought they should. It often
just hardened them more. "Surely we're here for
some reason," she wrote about her prison visits
with her husband. "There ought to be some way
for redemption for these men."

Inside the large mess hall, where the concert
took place, more than 1,000 men were crammed
into the room. It was packed denser than
Folsom Prison and the men seemed lustier,
more on edge, than at the previous taped show.
Violence seemed just a shout away, several of the
participants later would remark. You can hear it
in the inmates' shouts and responses, too. It was
a much rowdier, noisier crowd than on the
previous prison album.

Cash's manager, Lou Robin, asked the head of
security if he was sure there were enough guards
on hand to control such a teeming, heaving
crowd. "He pointed out that if he were to use
100 guards that night and the situation got out
of control, those 100 guards, or even another
100, wouldn't be able to do much," Robin said.

Once again, Cash delivered a concert with a
profane, rough edge that differed from his usual

shows. He seemed to respond to the inmates as much as they did to him. "June said she knew there'd be some people from the South here tonight," he said after the opening song, *Big River*. "Some of you guys get out here in California and it's so damn crazy you just got to get something to eat someway."

At another point, while tuning his guitar, the newly sober Cash jokes, "Hey, back there in my kit where I've got all my dope ... I mean all my things, there's a little red notebook if one of the guards can bring it to me. Yeah, you know that briefcase back there with all the songs I stole in it!"

He also presented an almost completely different set of songs than those he performed at Folsom — spurred, no doubt, by the fact that the show was being recorded. He did sing *I Still Miss Someone* again, though it didn't make the original LP version of the live recording. It was included when the entire show was released on CD in 2000.

In some ways, the set is lighter-hearted than the death, drugs and prison themes that marked the Folsom album. Johnny and June sang *Darlin' Companion*, a bouncy tune written by John Sebastian of the rock band The Lovin' Spoonful. He included *Walk the Line, Ring of Fire* and the gospel song *Daddy Sang Bass* in this set, too.

He once again sang part of a song written by an inmate. In this case, it's called *I Don't Know Where I'm Bound,* written by Thomas Cuttie, but unlike Glen Sherley's *Greystone Chapel,* this one didn't make the original recording. And he sang *Starkville City Jail,* based on the story of getting arrested for picking flowers while walking down the street in the Mississippi city, where it cost him $36 for breaking the town curfew.

It was an original song called *San Quentin* that really provoked the crowd, however.

"I tried to put myself in your place and I believe this is the way that I would feel about San Quentin," he said. The song's opening lines — *"San Quentin you've been living hell to me"* — raised a wild squall of sound from the crowd. *"You've cut me and you've scarred me through and through."* But the song addressed more than the pain and loneliness of the incarcerated. It also looked at the larger picture. *"San Quentin, what good do you think you do? Do you think I'll be different when you're through? You bend my heart and mind and you warp my soul, and your stone walls turn my blood a little cold."*

The crowd went berserk, shouting until he agreed to sing the song again. Before he did, Cash, sounding a bit hoarse, asked, "Hey, before we do it again, if any of the guards are still speaking to me, can I have a glass of water?" On the recording, you can hear how hard the inmates boo when the guard walks out with the refreshment.

After that, Cash calms the anger and fire he had stirred up with the song that would wind up being the most famous recorded that day. The decision to record *A Boy Named Sue* at the prison was rather spontaneous. Cash played the tape for Bob Johnston, the producer who recorded both the Folsom and San Quentin shows. Johnston thought it was funny and that the story song would go over well with the prisoners.

Cash didn't have time to memorize the lyrics, so he taped the words to the floor in front of his microphone stand. "I have a new song," he said, introducing it to the inmates. "I don't know it yet, but I'll sing it to you as best I can."

Using his larger-than-life persona to great comic effect, Cash sounds like he's having a blast performing the tale about a swaggering macho man improbably named Sue who tracks down the roustabout father who abandoned him at birth.

When Cash sings the opening lines, *"Well my Daddy left home when I was 3, and he didn't leave much to Ma and me, just this old guitar and an empty bottle of booze,"* the crowd immediately howls. *"I don't blame him 'cause he run and hid, but the meanest thing that he ever did, before he left he went and named me Sue."*

From the sound of the reaction, it must've already been obvious to Cash that he made the right choice in premiering the song before the inmates. Their reaction gave him energy and he added an extra level of animated drama to the narrative. He went on, telling the crowd that his dad must've had quite a laugh giving him a girl's name before leaving and that he ended up fighting his way through life due to all the guys who picked on him and tease him because of it.

"I'll tell ya, life ain't easy for a boy named Sue," Cash sang, his smirk obvious in the way he translates the lyrics. *"Well, I grew up quick and I grew up mean, my fists got hard and my wits got keen and I roamed from town to town to hide my shame."*

The singer vowed to search the world's bars to find the dirty dog who gave him a girl's name. One day, in a Gatlinburg honky tonk, he walked in to get a beer and recognized his father from the old picture he was carrying. He walked up to the table and said, *"My name is Sue! How do you do?! Now you're going to die!"*

The song then describes a hellish, brutal fight that includes Sue getting his ear cut off and they bust up the bar until the father reaches for a gun, only the son draws his first. *"He sat there looking at me and I saw him smile. He said,*

'Son, this world is rough, and if a man is going
to make it, he's gotta be tough. And I knew I
wouldn't be there to help you along. So I gave
you that name and I said goodbye, and I knew
you'd have to get tough or die.' "

The inmates howled at every stopped breath.
As Cash explains it, the father tells his son that
he wouldn't blame the younger man for killing
him. But he thinks Sue ought to thank him for
giving the boy a name that turned him into a
survivor. In the end, they hug, cry and reunite as
family. And Cash ends the song by crowing, "*If
I ever have a son, I think I'm gonna name him
... Bill or George or any damn thing but Sue. I
still hate that name!*"

The guys at San Quentin gave the song a
hero's welcome and, if anyone asked, they
would have said that the song was going to be a
smash hit.

Years later, Cash described *A Boy Named Sue*
as the one song he wished he never had to sing
again. "It's a hard song to do right," he said. "It's
an acting job. I have to play the father and the
son, and you really have to be up for it. There was
a live audience there when it was recorded and
it was new. The laughs were spontaneous. Now
everyone knows what's coming, so it's hard to get
a real reaction. I still try to do it every show."

The hit does highlight one aspect of Cash's

career: Even his novelty songs carry an underlying theme of hardship.

Cash also sings *Wanted Man*, which, as he tells the crowd, he wrote the previous week with Bob Dylan at his house in Hendersonville. But just as touching as anything on the album is Cash's transcendent version of the old country gospel tune, *Peace in the Valley*, which he sang at his brother Jack's funeral in 1944, and which, on the record, includes a beautiful harmony by the Carter Family.

As with all of Cash's material presented in the prison shows, it wasn't a random choice. He meant the message to be heard by those who were hanging on his every word in the mess hall that day. "*Well, the bear will be gentle, and the wolf will be tamed, and the lion shall lay down by the lamb,*" Cash intones with quiet deliberateness. "*And the beast from the wild will be led by a child, and I'll be changed from this creature, this creature that I am.*" The applause, while not as lusty as on other songs, goes on and on, as if the crowd wants to hold onto those words as long as they can.

Later in the show, Cash told the inmates of his trip to Israel earlier in the year with June. "There are some things in this world that everybody wants to see or hear at one point or another in their lives and, especially for you fellows, we'd

Young Johnny Cash (right) in an Arkansas cottonfield with his older brother Jack and sister Reba.

"God has his hand on you," Carrie Cash told her son Johnny when she heard him sing. She predicted that one day he'd be a country music star. Soldier of Fortune: Johnny Cash began performing while stationed in Germany with the U.S. Air Force.

The Tennessee Two: Johnny Cash with his bandmates, Marshall Grant (left) on bass and Luther Perkins on electric guitar.

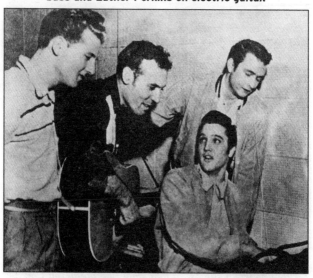

The Million Dollar Quartet: Jerry Lee Lewis (left), Carl Perkins and Johnny Cash flank Elvis Presley at the piano in Sun Studios.

Country comedian Minnie Pearl cuts up with Cash on his first visit to the Grand Ole Opry in 1956. "I never played much rock 'n' roll 'cause I got so much country in my soul," Cash once wrote in a song. The performer, (below left) with manager S. Holif and future wife June Carter, said he fell in love with June the moment he met her. The Country Rebel: Cash, with Grand Ole Opry stalwart Ernest Tubb, brought a new sound to country music.

*The dark prince of country music visits
with the king of rock 'n' roll, Elvis Presley.*

Johnny Cash at home with his first wife Vivian and his daughters Kathleen and Rosanne (holding the guitar). He'd later express regret at how his drug abuse separated him from his duties as a family man and father.

Cash was arrested in El Paso, Texas, in 1965 for buying a large quantity of pills in Juarez, Mexico. It would be his seventh and final arrest before kicking his drug habit.

"We got married in a fever, hotter than a pepper sprout," Johnny and June Carter sang in their hit song "Jackson."

The Class of '55: Johnny Cash, Carl Perkins (center) and Jerry Lee Lewis share a laugh backstage, two decades after the three men started their careers in Memphis at Sun Records in 1955.

Cash performs at Cummins Prison Farm in Arkansas. "By doing prison concerts, we were letting inmates know that somewhere out there in the free world was somebody who cared for them as human beings."

The jokers are wild: Johnny Cash and country music rabble-rouser Roger Miller crack up on stage during a segment of "The Johnny Cash Show."

Rags to riches: Cash and his friend and bandmate Carl Perkins were both sons of Depression-era sharecroppers. "I was able to work with some great talent who were guests on the show," Cash said. "And I was able to have many of my friends on the show, and many more who became friends," such as rhythm-and-blues great Ray Charles.

The Man in Black loved the "Ride This Train" segment of his hit TV variety show.

Cash stirred up a controversy when he refused to perform two songs requested by President Richard Nixon that weren't his. All was forgiven when Nixon, with first lady Pat, joked about it with him and June Carter Cash.

Cash, Merle Haggard and Buck Owens join the host of the "Glen Campbell Goodtime Hour."

Cash with Country Music Hall of Fame members
Tex Ritter (left) and Roy Acuff. Later, when Cash was
inducted into the Hall of Fame, he said, "It's the stylists
that have made country music what it is today."

Among the many stars who appeared with Cash were
country-pop singer Sonny James, who headlined the first
concert Cash played as a Sun Records artist in 1955, and
Tammy Wynette, still a legend-in-the-making in 1971 after
such hits as "Stand By Your Man" and "D-I-V-O-R-C-E."

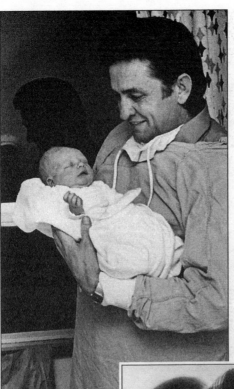

The proud papa beams as he cradles his newborn son, John Carter Cash, in 1970.

June Carter Cash helped her husband conquer his drug habit.

Actor Kirk Douglas brawls with Cash in a scene from the 1971 film, "A Gunfight."

In 2002 the pair was reunited when they accepted their National Medals of Arts during a ceremony hosted by President George W. Bush.

Kirk Douglas and Johnny Cash were all smiles on the set of "A Gunfight."

The happy family arrives in Tel Aviv to begin work on their ambitious religious project, "The Gospel Road," which attempted to follow the footsteps of Jesus Christ in the Holy Land. Cash testifies in a Senate Subcommittee hearing on prison reform (below). "San Quentin is a hellhole," Cash said of the famous California prison where he often performed. "It ought to rot and burn in hell for all the good it does."

John Carter Cash, with help from his Dad, makes his Las Vegas debut at age 3, singing "Mary Had a Little Lamb." When John Carter was born, Cash pledged to be a better father than he had been with his four daughters.

Kris Kristofferson, who wrote Cash's No. 1 hit "Sunday Morning Coming Down," once described the singer as "a walking contradiction, partly truth and partly fiction." The Man in Black stands in his Tennessee home with a silver-plated six shooter and a prized Remington bronze sculpture.

During one of his many trips to Israel during the '70s and '80s, Cash poses in front of the Wailing Wall in Jerusalem.

The Cash family album: With his parents Ray and Carrie
Cash in the center, Johnny poses with all his brothers,
sisters, children, nieces and nephews at a family reunion
that the singer suggested and helped organize.

Tall in the saddle: Cash carried a lifelong special interest in the Old West and cowboy lore. Here he rides horseback for a segment of a 1982 CBS-TV special.

Cash dances while listening to a musical performance in Hiltons, Virginia, where June's cousins maintained a folk music venue in honor of their parents.

Willie Nelson, Kris Kristofferson, Waylon Jennings and Cash perform as The Highwaymen. The supergroup formed after Cash asked the others to join him for a TV special. "We had so much fun," he said, "we decided to make a habit of it."

All my rowdy friends: Cash with longtime pal Waylon Jennings (left) and Hank Williams Jr., the godson of June Carter Cash.

The Man in Black, as ominous, foreboding and imposing as ever (above). Those who knew Cash best spoke of his uninhibited sense of humor – a side of himself he rarely revealed in public, but one that obviously shows through in this mid-'80s photograph.

All in the family: John Carter Cash, Carlene Carter, Johnny Cash, Rosanne Cash and June Carter Cash. Though all three children of the Cash-Carter clan pictured here came from different pairings, Johnny and June refused to ever use the word "stepchild." "They're all our children," June liked to say.

Heroes and legends: The Cashes with their close friend Rev. Billy Graham (center) with the famous Western couple Dale Evans and Roy Rogers, the King of the Cowboys.

Cash performs at a tribute in his honor with (from left) Trisha Yearwood, Chris Isaak, June Carter Cash, Kris Kristofferson and Sheryl Crow.

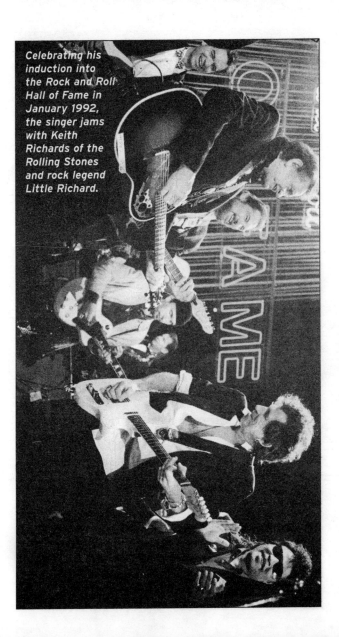

Celebrating his induction into the Rock and Roll Hall of Fame in January 1992, the singer jams with Keith Richards of the Rolling Stones and rock legend Little Richard.

Cash and Bob Dylan became friends in the early 1960s when the Man in Black defended the groundbreaking songwriter and began recording his songs. Rick Rubin, producer of Run D.M.C. and the Red Hot Chili Peppers, helped Cash resurrect his career in the '90s by signing him to American Records and collaborating on a series of critically acclaimed, Grammy-winning albums. Rocker Tom Petty and his band, the Heartbreakers, provided musical support for "Unchained," Cash's second album for American Records. Of Cash and longtime pal Waylon Jennings (above), June Carter Cash once said: "They've been through hell and high water together."

Plagued by various health problems, Cash had been in and out of the hospital for the last few years, yet he never stopped making music.

The Man in Black leans into the casket of his wife, June Carter Cash, to say goodbye.

His daughter Rosanne said, "My father has lost his greatest companion, his musical partner and his soul mate." Late in life, Cash said of his wife: "She's the easiest woman in the world for me to live with, I guess because I know her so well and she knows me so well. We've both found our place where we totally belong, in every avenue of endeavor."

In his final public appearance, Cash performed at the Carter Family Fold in Hiltons, Virginia, in June 2003 – just a month after the death of his wife. Before singing the gospel song "Angel Band," he said, "Baby, I know you're here with me tonight."

Flowers and other mementos rest on Johnny Cash's Hollywood Walk of Fame star. "Johnny represented the best of America," said his friend Kris Kristofferson, "and we won't see his likes again."

feel good if we could bring back sounds of the people and the places. I know for a lot of you, you're a lot like I was; they were always dear to you, the stories and the sounds of Israel. We went to Nazareth, we went to the Sea of Galilee, we went to Jerusalem, to the Way of the Cross, to the Wailing Wall."

He tells of going into Canaan to a church with a cistern where the water came from that Jesus turned into wine, where the first miracle was performed. "I was so impressed, coming out of the church, if I've ever had an inspiration, I had one then, from seeing what I'd just seen and heard," Cash said. He related to the prisoners how he wrote a new gospel song that day, *He Turned the Water Into Wine*.

It's interesting to hear the change in the crowd. The men who started out so violent and lustful were now clapping, shouting, celebrating Cash's convergence from the raging rebel who opened the show to the transformed man who presented his testimony at the close of the concert.

By the time the group broke into *Daddy Sang Bass* — "a song about the reason for it all," Cash says — you can hear a room full of inmates clapping and singing and rejoicing along with the Man in Black about how *"singing seems to help a troubled soul."* As the song hits the chorus, there's Mother Maybelle and the rest of the

Carters harmonizing with him, *"No, the circle won't be broken, by and by, Lord, by and by."*

From there, they all — the people on stage, the men in the audience — keep clapping and singing, slipping right into another gospel tune, *The Old Account Was Settled Long Ago* and by then Cash no longer is identifying with the anger and frustration of the criminals who've been imprisoned. By the end of the show, he's testifying to a congregation and they're worshipping right along with him. It's one of the more remarkable live recording experiences ever caught on record.

The live version of *A Boy Named Sue* was released in July 1969 by Columbia Records and it became a runaway No. 1 hit. It sold 3 million copies as a single and the Country Music Association crowned it Single of the Year for 1969. The song's unlikely success pushed the sales of "Johnny Cash at San Quentin" to more than 6 million copies, reaching even greater heights than the Folsom Prison album, once again setting new sales records for a country album. It also was his only album ever to reach No. 1 on the Billboard popular album charts and it stayed there for four consecutive weeks.

The San Quentin show also provided the backdrop for one of the most famous photographs of Johnny Cash. It shows him with a furious snarl on his face, bending and thrusting a middle finger toward the camera.

Apparently, sometime during the show, the TV crew filming the event began crowding the front of the stage. Cash felt it interfered with his connection with the inmates and he asked the crew to clear the way, because he couldn't see the audience with everyone filling the gap in front of the stage. When no one moved, Cash pushed his microphone stand aside, stepped forcefully toward the crew and expressed his displeasure by giving them the universal signal. Rock 'n' roll photographer Jim Marshall, who was also documenting the event for Columbia Records, perfectly captured the awesome fury of Cash when scorned.

Later, when asked why he thought the prison concerts were his most popular albums and why he had such success with songs about murderers and prisoners, Cash said, "You know, the biggest song of the 19th century was about Jesse James. The whole country was singing the praises of Jesse James. It's always been an American theme to make heroes out of the criminals. Right or wrong, we've always done it. You know, it really is a crime in itself, but we do it. I think there's a little bit of criminal in all of us. Everybody's done something wrong they don't want anybody to know about. Maybe that's where it comes from."

15

The prison concerts proved to be a lasting high-water mark in the career of Johnny Cash. Another came when ABC-TV asked if he wanted to host his own variety show. "We felt right about it as an opportunity to do the music we loved doing and to do it for millions of people," Cash wrote in *Man in Black*. "I enjoyed the television shows, for the most part. I was able to work with some great talent who were guests on the show and I was able to have many of my friends on the show and many more who became friends."

The first night of taping for *The Johnny Cash Show*, the singer walked out onto the stage at the Ryman Auditorium and received a standing ovation. It was a clear sign of how far he'd come. Just four years earlier, he was kicked off the *Grand Ole Opry* after his drug-induced fit led to his breaking all the stage lights. Now here he was, bringing country music to the nation from the same stage. When he walked off after finishing the program, the first hand he shook belonged to the same *Opry* manager who had fired him. "That was one of the greatest joys of my career," he wrote.

The show broke ground in the way it combined hip young singer-songwriters, country stars and musicians from other walks of life. Guests included such rockers as Bob Dylan, Neil Young, Joni Mitchell and Linda Ronstadt as well as country stars like Merle Haggard, Roger Miller and Charley Pride. Everyone from Liza Minnelli to gospel star Mahalia Jackson performed. The show always closed with a hymn, usually one that found the Carter Family, the Statler Brothers and Carl Perkins joining Cash onstage to sing.

He also included a "Ride This Train" segment

in each show. It allowed Cash to indulge his love of history, as the segment would show him riding the rails to some historic American location, where he discussed what happened there and why it was important to U.S. history. "That show made country music hip to a lot of people who had never paid attention to it before," said Kris Kristofferson.

Kristofferson was in Nashville for four years when he finally persuaded his idol, Johnny Cash, to cut one of his songs. He struggled through jobs as a janitor, a bartender and a helicopter pilot before finally starting to gain some success as a Nashville songwriter. Roger Miller had just cut *Me and Bobby McGee*, making it a country hit two years before Janis Joplin recorded the most famous version of the tune.

Inspired, Kristofferson set his sights on Cash. The two first met backstage at the *Grand Ole Opry* in 1965 and Cash was encouraging to Kristofferson, who at the time was a U.S. Army captain and a member of the elite Airborne Rangers. Kristofferson, also a Rhodes Scholar who had a degree in English literature from Oxford University, was appointed to be a literature professor at West Point. But before taking his new job, he traveled to Nashville on a whim while hiding a secret desire to write country songs full time.

His chance meeting with Cash helped convince Kristofferson to move to Nashville, bringing his wife and two children with him. Four years later, Kristofferson had nothing left to lose. His wife divorced him and most of his family disowned him.

The songwriter had tried to get to Cash once before, busting in on a recording session at Columbia Studios to give the Man in Black a tape of his songs. The move almost got Kristofferson fired from his job as the studio's janitorial assistant.

Cash later remembered accepting the tape from the scruffy former army captain, but he didn't remember if he had ever listened to it or not.

This time Kristofferson, now picking up money as a member of the National Guard, decided he needed to make a stronger impression on the Man in Black.

June Carter Cash always told the story best. She remembered hearing a horrendously loud sound at the couple's Hendersonville home on Old Hickory Lake. She looked out to see a helicopter lowering down to land on a lakefront bluff on the couple's property. She went to wake up her husband, who was taking a nap. "John," she said. "The tourists have been coming by boat and by bus, but now they're coming by air."

Kristofferson clutched a tape that included a song, *Sunday Morning Coming Down*. Cash met the younger man as he walked across the large yard. Cash took the tape and angrily pitched it into the lake and ordered Kristofferson to get the hell off his property.

Ray Stevens ended up cutting the song first, but Cash eventually heard it. He decided to perform it on his TV show, only the network censors objected. Full of language and images not previously heard in a country song, it told of an alcoholic waking up alone and hung-over on a bright Sunday morning full of happy families and inviting homes. The producers tied their objection to one line: *"On a Sunday morning sidewalk, wishing Lord that I was stoned."*

Kristofferson attended the rehearsal where the producers and Cash debated the line, and the producers offered the singer alternate lines. Cash said he'd have to think about it — and the producers told him they couldn't air the song if he didn't change it.

Kristofferson sat in the Ryman balcony during the taping and when Cash reached the line in question, he looked straight at Kristofferson and sang the words as they were written. It was featured in the TV show and, to everyone's surprise, the live version from the TV show became a No. 1 hit.

The following year, Kristofferson won Song of the Year honors at the Country Music Association Awards. Within another year, the once destitute songwriter had his own record deal. And within two years, he was appearing in his first Hollywood movie. Cash had undoubtedly set him on his career path by taking a chance with an edgy, outspoken song.

The popular show gave Cash's career yet another jolt and he proved more successful than ever. He also felt more secure about himself and his life, with his marriage to June and his faith holding up strong. Thousands of fan letters poured in every week. Cash bought a second large home in Hendersonville, this one on Gallatin Pike, about a mile from the Old Hickory Lake mansion. In the second home he opened the House of Cash recording studio, which June decorated in blue. (It would later become a museum filled with Cash memorabilia.) His sister Reba Hancock moved back from California to manage the studio and to handle his public relations.

With the show a hit and home life feeling more blissful all the time, Johnny and June decided to have a child. For a few months they were unsuccessful. So Johnny booked a vacation to the Virgin Islands, hoping the relaxation would do them both some good — and perhaps give them the going-away gift they were hoping to receive. It was a magical time, Cash would later say. On the flight home, he turned to June and said, "Let's name him John Carter Cash." June, flabbergasted, blurted back, "What makes you think I'm pregnant?"

"I just believe you are," Johnny said with a smile. A few weeks later, June began experiencing morning sickness. She visited the doctor and when she returned home, Cash was waiting, expectantly. "I believe I am, too," June told him. "What?" Cash asked excitedly. "Pregnant," she said coyly and then they screamed and hugged.

When John Carter Cash was born, his father pledged to be a better father than he was with his four daughters. He saw it as another chance and he planned to make the best of it.

His controversies weren't over — they rarely are when a star becomes as big as Johnny Cash was in 1969. President Richard Nixon invited Cash to perform at the White House, a request the singer felt honored to receive. Three days before the show, his sister Reba Hancock called to say he had received three song requests for the evening performance.

Surprised, Cash asked what they were. Two weren't even his songs. *A Boy Named Sue* seemed natural enough, but he had also been asked to sing Merle Haggard's *Okie from Muskogee* and a song called *Welfare Cadillac*, a hit for singer Guy Drake about people taking advantage of social assistance.

Cash told his sister to call the White House back and say he couldn't perform those two songs. Robert Haldeman, the president's chief of staff, called to say that was fine. But by the time Cash arrived in Washington, the press corps had found out that he turned down a request from the President of the United States.

Nixon, fortunately, laughed it off. When introducing the singer, Nixon mentioned that John Carter Cash was upstairs asleep in the Lincoln bedroom. And he said that he had found out that he didn't know Cash's song catalog as well as he should have. The president, his aides and the guests received Cash's program of old hits and gospel songs well.

16

With his TV show doing well, Cash took on his first truly serious acting role, starring in *A Gunfight* with actor Kirk Douglas. The film was the first major American motion picture to be produced by an Indian tribe, the Jicarilla Apaches of New Mexico. Cash starred as Abe and Douglas as Will, two aging, famous gunfighters past their prime and penniless. So they scheme up a way to make a big score: They decide to stage a gunfight between themselves and sell tickets.

Douglas' character is set up as the clear favorite, but he has his doubts. He knows Cash's Abe is a capable quick draw. The ending is set up as a surprise, showing how one life would play out if he won, before turning the tables on the audience. At the time, the movie, with its humiliation and brutalization of both gunfighters, was seen as an allegory about the crass commercialization of the Old West.

Cash also began regular appearances across America on the *Billy Graham Crusades*. As Cash began speaking about his renewed faith and how Christianity helped him get over his addictions and gave him a new vigor for life, he suddenly found himself deluged with requests to perform at benefits or to help people in one way or another. The letters often would begin "God told me to write you" or that God sent them to the singer for assistance.

Guilty about his own wealth and his own sins, at first Cash tried to help whenever he could. But soon the requests overwhelmed him. There wasn't nearly enough time or money for him to do all he was asked to do. He eventually had to hire a security guard for his home to keep tourists, curiosity seekers and those looking for help from coming to his door.

The guard apparently had a sense of humor. Once, a man came to Cash's gate while the singer was on a concert tour. "The Lord sent me to see Johnny Cash," the man told the guard. "Didn't the Lord tell you Johnny Cash was in Pittsburgh?" the guard replied.

Still, the tour buses came, sometimes as many as 40 or 50 a day passing down the small, barely two-lane road that led to the Cash compound. Whenever Johnny or June had to leave the house, they had to leave early so that they could spend time at the gate signing autographs and posing for photos with the fans who had gathered.

There were scary incidents, however. The most frightening came when Rosie Carter, barely into her teens, walked in and found a stranger standing in her bedroom. She froze, petrified, and called out for her stepfather. The man assured Rosie he wouldn't hurt her, but he had a glassy, stoned look in his eyes.

Cash hurried in. "Who are you and how did you get in here?" the patriarch asked. "I slipped in," the stranger responded. "The door was open. You don't know me." Cash grabbed him in a headlock and dragged him to the front door. He shoved him out and the man fell to the ground, then jumped up and high-tailed it out of there.

Cash moved his parents to Hendersonville as well, putting them up in a stately new home not far from his own. But they, too, were hounded by fans and charity seekers, who knocked on the door all hours of the day and night with requests for photographs or information about their famous son. Cash came to a conclusion: "I decided if I did my best, followed my conscience, took care of my home and family, and prayed daily for wisdom to know what to do, then I need not worry."

Cash won a host of Grammy and Country Music Association Awards in 1970, thanks to the success of *A Boy Named Sue*. He hit the 1970s on a great roll. He had recently recorded a series of songs that would rank with his most enduring works: *Jackson, Rosanna's Running Wild, Daddy Sang Bass, A Boy Named Sue, If I Were a Carpenter, Sunday Morning Coming Down, Flesh and Blood* and *Man in Black* were all released in the fertile period between 1967 and 1972. Moreover, his concert fee had climbed higher and the bookings got larger and better. He performed at the Hollywood Bowl, Carnegie Hall and other top venues.

He was invited to New York's Waldorf-Astoria hotel for a party honoring Mamie Eisenhower, the former first lady. Bob Hope, Bing Crosby, Raquel Welch, senators, congressman, generals and other politicians and celebrities also attended the televised event. Cash rehearsed a six-minute

medley of songs for the show and the warm-up
went great.

But, prior to the show, he was asked to attend
a black-tie cocktail event. He always hated
those kinds of social parties, he felt frazzled and
upset by all the phoniness.

Then, during his live portion of the program,
he dropped his pick just as he hit the first
strummed note on his guitar. He bent to pick it
up and his black trousers ripped from the knee to
the crotch. The rip happened to the inner right
leg and Mamie Eisenhower was seated to his left.
She clearly saw it and she blushed and tried not
to laugh. Cash, embarrassed, hurried through his
song while others in the crowd giggled. Then he
rushed off stage.

Back at his hotel suite, he threw a fit, tearing
off his clothes and hiding in the bathroom. When
he finally came out, June sat there, staring at him
for a few minutes before she cracked up in laughter. Cash angrily asked her what could possibly
be so funny. "John," she told him, "tonight the
Lord busted your britches!" Cash, too, fell over in
laughter and the couple rolled on the hotel floor
in each other's arms, laughing so hard they could
hardly stop.

As well as things were going, Cash also decided
it was time to stop smoking. He began smoking
when he was 12 years old, back when his brother

Jack was still alive, so the habit had been with him a long time. But he got inspired to quit during a time when his son John Carter was hospitalized with a bad cold. They put the baby boy in an oxygen tent and Cash would lie with him. But every time the singer coughed, the boy woke up and cried.

A doctor heard the cough and encouraged Cash to quit, explaining that the hospital had a program that could help him. For two hours a day for five days, Cash attended the seminar. By Friday night, on April 23, 1970, he was done with smoking. But it wasn't easy; after all, he had the habit for 30 years. He dreamed of cigarettes at night, he later said. After about a month, the cravings stopped.

As he neared the end of taping the second season of his TV show, Cash ran into problems with the New York producers. They protested when he confessed his Christian faith during a segment while introducing a gospel song. He was receiving letters, asking him if he was a "true" Christian or not, since he always closed with a gospel number. He decided to end the speculation with a public statement of faith.

One of the producers told him he shouldn't talk about religion, God or Jesus on national TV. Cash didn't take kindly to that. He never did like it when an executive or producer — be it

Sam Phillips or a New York TV exec — told him to put Christian music or pronouncements behind him.

"Well, then, you're producing the wrong man here," Cash responded. "The word 'gospel' means 'the good news about Jesus Christ' and gospel music is a part of what I am and part of what I do. I don't cram anything down people's throats, but neither do I make any apologies for it. In a song introduction, I have to tell it like it is. I'm not going to proselytize and I'm not going to compromise. So don't you worry about me mentioning Jesus, or God, or Moses, or whoever I decide to mention in the spiritual realm. If you don't like it, you can always edit it."

Cash also reacted badly when the producers took a stronger hand in booking guests, many of whom had little in common with the host. When the producers let him know that they planned to cut his train segment, Cash blew up. He told them he didn't want to do the show unless he had a greater say in his guest stars and if he could keep segments of integrity and truth like "Ride This Train." The show wasn't renewed.

He made the best of his final shows. He introduced one of his most famous songs, *Man in Black*, on the second-to-last program. The song explained an oft-asked question about Cash's monochrome taste in clothing. *"I wear the black for the poor and beaten down,"* the song says, and went on to list prisoners, the sick, the old, the unsaved as those he represented, too, and that he would continue to wear black until the world became a brighter, happier, more just place for all. His final show was an all-gospel program that the producers didn't want. But Cash insisted. His guests included the Oak Ridge Boys, the Blackwood Brothers, Mahalia Jackson, Stuart Hamblin and Rev. Billy Graham. "The whole show was a closing hymn," he said.

By the time Billy Graham appeared on Cash's show, the two men — both of them Southern icons, but of a completely different type — had become close friends. That might surprise people; it certainly would've shocked them had it happened a few years earlier, when Cash was in and out of jail. Graham initiated the friendship. Out of the blue, the preacher called the singer to ask if he could visit the Cash home. The Man in Black extended the invitation. Graham came to dinner and spent the night, and he had locked into conversation with Johnny and June throughout the evening. Graham never mentioned Cash appearing on one of his crusades, but Cash did. He offered to perform, if Graham would allow it. They became regulars on the big, stadium-filling events that Graham staged to save souls and convert new believers.

17

Even though his TV show had ended, Cash was at the height of his success. That meant he had more leverage than ever, but it also meant he had more to lose than ever before. And it was at this point that he took the biggest gamble of his career: He and June poured millions of dollars into a project they called *The Gospel Road*. It was first and foremost a movie, though it also came to encompass an album and book as well.

The Cashes came to believe the project would fulfill the premonition June had in a dream the first time the couple visited Israel three years earlier. "I talked to people in all walks of religious life," Cash wrote of the plans. "I hungered for a broader understanding of the chosen people and found their faith as diversified as Christian denominations."

As Cash explained, *Gospel Road* would use his music as an identification point, but its primary mission was to be an expression of their faith — "our witness and testimony and the overshadowing power in it will be the words of Jesus."

A potential national sponsor backed out when the company asked for a script; Cash said there wasn't one and he didn't plan to create one because he didn't want anyone looking over his shoulder with the power to influence or veto any creative decisions. He later said he was happy that the sponsor backed out.

The couple hired a documentary filmmaker, Robert Elfstrom, who also would play Christ in the film. June, who was trained as an actor at New York's Neighborhood Playhouse in the '50s, played Mary Magdalene. The story was to follow the life of Christ and it was shot with the assistance of the Israeli government, which provided security and passage to holy sights. A primary location was Mount Arabel, a beautiful peak above Tiberias and overlooking Galilee. They finished the bulk of the shoot in 30 days and returned to Tennessee.

Later, as the film was edited, Cash wrote new songs for the soundtrack and added narration. The soundtrack also included songs by the Statler Brothers, who launched their own career separate from their work with Cash, and a newcomer named Larry Gatlin who was soon to become a country star. Gatlin's contributions included *Help Me*, a song Cash first heard Gatlin sing in church. Meanwhile, Kristofferson wrote a gospel song, too, and wanted June and Johnny to hear it. The song, *Why Me (Lord)?*, made June weep and it went on to become one of Kristofferson's most recorded tunes.

By the time *The Gospel Road* was ready for release, it was 1973. Twentieth Century Fox made a bid to distribute the film, but admitted upfront that they weren't sure how to market a religious movie. Cash traveled the country as the movie opened, making personal appearances at openings and doing every interview he could.

Just as June dreamed, the movie opens with Cash standing on a mountaintop, a Bible in his hand and he's talking about Jesus Christ. Just as June dreamed, millions of people saw and heard him. Still, the movie struggled to get into theaters, though it often did well in those that agreed to show it. Eventually, Rev. Billy Graham stepped in to help, agreeing to have his company World Wide distribute the film. "We know its audience," Graham told Cash. After that, the film was shown to packed churches across the United States.

Amid all the success and celebration, the Cashes got startling news one day while resting in their new home in the farming community of Bon Aqua, Tennessee. The couple usually went there for some peace and quiet, to escape the tourists and hectic life of their Hendersonville home. Johnny's sister Reba took John Carter, his cousin Kevin Jones and a carload of friends out riding through the Cash property in a top-down Jeep. After more than an hour of bumping around the meadows, the Jeep hit some loose rocks and turned over.

A tour bus just happened to be coming up the drive and the passengers saw the accident. The bus unloaded and they ran to help turn the Jeep back on its wheels. Several of the children were seriously injured, including John Carter. The Cashes rushed to Madison Hospital, but by the time they arrived, John Carter had been transferred to the intensive care unit at Vanderbilt Hospital in midtown Nashville. June fell to her knees crying when she heard the news and they both feared the worst. Their friends and neighbors, Roy and Barbara Orbison, arrived and drove them to Vanderbilt. As they ran in the door, a doctor met them. He informed them that it wasn't as serious as it had first seemed. John Carter had a small skull fracture and a concussion.

Besides their Bon Aqua home, and a home in Port Richey, Florida, that June had inherited from her mother, the Cashes began traveling to Jamaica to get away from the hustle of their lives and to relax amid the ocean breezes and tall palms. In 1974, Johnny and June were vacationing in Jamaica as the guests of John Rollins, the former lieutenant governor of Delaware and owner of the Dover Downs casino and horse racing track, the large Rollins Truck Leasing companies and Rollins security firms.

While riding around in a four-wheeler with Rollins, Johnny saw the enormous, elegant Jamaican house that would soon become his favorite getaway spot. Named Cinnamon Hill, it's a limestone home with 4-foot-thick walls and solid mahogany doors built in 1747 on a cliff that sits 280 feet above sea level. The famous Barretts of Winpole Street, the family of the poet Elizabeth Barrett Browning, were the original owners.

Cash wanted to buy it that day from Rollins. The home needed renovation and Cash pledged to fix it up grandly. Rollins said Cash could renovate the home and use it anytime he wanted, but the businessman didn't want to sell it. Johnny agreed and turned the home back into the showcase it once had been. Johnny, June and John Carter first stayed in the house during the 1975 Christmas season. By then, Johnny was more determined than ever to buy it. Though Rollins was reluctant, the two families eventually settled on a price and Cinnamon Hill became part of the Cash family. "We've always put our money into land and property," Cash once said. "I never cared much about luxury items."

Meanwhile, Cash's success as a recording artist suddenly plunged. Perhaps it was because of all the time he had spent pursuing *The Gospel Road* and concentrating on his family life and his spiritual journey. But for whatever reason, he hadn't scored a No. 1 country song since 1971's *Flesh and Blood*. In 1973 and 1974, he didn't even achieved a Top 10 hit.

He couldn't blame anyone but himself. His songs lacked their usual inspiration. Single releases like *The World Needs a Melody, The Loving Gift, Praise the Lord and Pass the Soup, Allegheny, Lady from Baltimore* and *Orleans Parish Prison* weren't anywhere near his best work. After finishing the '60s on the strength of his prison albums and a couple of other strong collections ("Hello I'm Johnny Cash," "The Johnny Cash Show"), the '70s didn't create any Cash masterpieces.

Only a few years after the prison concerts, the TV show and such unforgettable songs as *Sunday Morning Coming Down* and *Man in Black*, Cash was no longer a force on the country music charts. But he still played to huge, sold-out audiences and he remained a popular guest star on TV specials and variety shows. He made a famous appearance on *Columbo*, a network detective series starring Peter Falk as an investigator who uses a bumbling personality to hide his sharp crime-solving skills. Cash starred as a country music singer who might be a murderer. He appeared in several other TV shows through the years and he seemed especially keen to act in Americana-type programs, such as *Little House on the Prairie*, *Davy Crockett* and *Dr. Quinn, Medicine Woman*.

In 1974, he recorded what he considered his least favorite album. Ironically, it was given the title "John R. Cash," but despite the namesake title, he felt it represented him less than anything he had ever created. CBS Records was concerned about his slipping sales and lack of radio exposure. They worried that he concentrated too much on gospel music and on songs recorded with June or with the Carter Family. They also thought he stayed so busy with everything that it left him little time to concentrate on finding or writing songs.

So they made him a deal: They wanted to choose a pile of songs they thought might interest him. They'd let him make the final choices. Then they'd record all the musical tracks and all he had to do is take a few days to sing the lyrics.

That's how it was done and it was not an unusual process in the modern recording business. But Cash hated it. He *enjoyed* being involved in the arrangements, in the grit of making an album. He felt disconnected from the material and the music, and it showed in the recording. He didn't get a single hit from the album, so it failed to please the record company as well. He never recorded another album in that fashion.

Cash described his first autobiography, *Man in Black*, as "a spiritual odyssey." He spent more than nine months writing the book in longhand and an experienced writer, Peter Gillquist, guided him with questions and helped shape his writing into paragraphs and chapters, "correcting my 1950 high school English grammar along the way."

Painstakingly describing his own descent into the hell of substance abuse, he wrote the book to encourage those facing the same problems he fought and to give strength to fellow Christians who got caught up in their own personal crises.

Meanwhile, his health, after several years of recovery, was the best it had been in some time. Following a physical, his doctor told him, "I'd say you were about 25 years old, if I didn't know better."

Cash realized that, after he converted to a stronger faith, some of his friends missed his wilder side. They criticized him for "getting religion," as he wrote in *Man in Black*. They believed that his music, which had grown more spiritual, lacked the raw intensity of his earlier songs. Cash didn't deny that he was a different man. "If you're going to be a Christian, you're going to change," he wrote. "You're going to lose some old friends, not because you want to, but because you need to. You can't compromise some things."

He even enrolled in a college correspondence course on the Bible. He joined about 20 people in the study class, meeting every Monday night to talk about their current readings. When Cash missed a class because of his travel schedule, he mailed in his lessons.

He explained his reasons for the study class this way: "One reason is to satisfy my hunger for a deeper understanding, a richer knowledge and a closer walk with the Lord. Another reason is my love for history and, after three trips to

Israel, especially my love of the history of the Jews. But mainly I feel that the studies are necessary for experiencing the spiritual growth I need so badly."

Meanwhile, the Cashes, especially June, continued to provide help for those in need. June's friend Audrey Williams, was near death and asked June to always look after her famous son, Hank Williams Jr. But Hank Jr. grew wilder in the mid-1970s, hanging out with Southern rockers, boasting in song of how much whiskey he could drink, how much pot he could smoke and how many women he could have.

But Hank Jr.'s biggest crisis didn't come from substance abuse. He was hunting elk on a Montana mountainside in 1975 when he fell down a rugged slope, bouncing harshly off of jagged boulders as he tumbled down. He nearly died right there, his face shattered, with bones broken, tissue exposed, his forehead ripped back completely. The Cashes rushed to his side in an intensive care unit. June stayed with him as he persevered through long hospital stays and extensive facial surgeries.

18

Cash finally found his way back onto country radio in 1976 and it took another jive novelty song to get him there. *One Piece at a Time* might not have carried the cleverness or the weight of *A Boy Named Sue*. But it was a funny, light-hearted take on a factory worker who tried to build himself a free Cadillac by stealing different parts *"one piece at a time,"* as the title states. The joke was that he ended up with a misshapen mismatch of parts that didn't go together, making the car a wild, contorted vehicle unlike anything anyone had ever seen. It became his first No. 1 hit in five years. It was also his last as a solo artist. The only other No. 1 in the rest of his career was with *The Highwayman*, which he recorded with friends Willie Nelson, Waylon Jennings and Kris Kristofferson.

Despite his recent hit record, Cash still seemed creatively adrift, putting out one ignored album after another. He and CBS kept trying to find a new formula, though. His 1977 album "Rambler" is one that Cash always felt proud of; even though it didn't sell well, nor did it produce any big hits. The concept is that he's driving across America, picking up hitchhikers and the dialogue centers on the conversations he has with them. Cash blamed the record company's lack of marketing for its failure.

By 1978, he tried to align himself with the booming outlaw movement. After all, the artists who led the charge — Willie Nelson, Waylon Jennings, Tompall Glaser, Billy Joe Shaver, etc. — were all strongly influenced by Cash and connected to him by artistic vision and musical direction. On the album "I Would Like to See You Again," one of the decade's better efforts, he offers a couple of duets with Jennings (*I Wish I Was Crazy Again, There Ain't No Good Chain*

Gang), as well as a handful of other strong tunes. But the album failed to connect with the young rockers attracted to the outlaw bunch and it did no better with country's core audience.

Another attempt at reviving his career by updating his sound came with 1979's "Silver," which features Emmylou Harris' producer and ex-husband Brian Ahern leading the sessions. It was an earnest attempt at finding a way to make Cash sound fresh and this time they didn't force the veteran singer into anything that made him uncomfortable. Ahern and Harris spent time at Cinnamon Hill with the Cashes, becoming friends who were at ease around each other. The song selection was also more inventive, with cuts like *The L&N Don't Stop Here Anymor*e and the classic *Ghost Riders in the Sky*, which hit No. 2 on the radio charts. Still, the album didn't kick up Cash's sales, nor did it make him sound more relevant or contemporary, which was the goal. Mostly the modernized arrangements only took away from the earthy power that is key to Cash's artistry.

The '80s and country music's *Urban Cowboy* boom that preceded it found Cash once again trying to instill new energy into his career. His 1980 album "Rockabilly Blues" was one of his best of the period. Most of it was produced by his pianist, Earl Poole Ball. Jack Clement also produced a track, as did Cash's new son-in-law, Nick Lowe, who married stepdaughter Carlene Carter. The British pub rocker was on a creative roll, producing the early Elvis Costello albums, putting out acclaimed solo albums and knocking out brilliant rock records with his collaborator Dave Edmunds in their band Rockpile.

On the album, the title track and *Cold Lonesome Morning* found Cash writing with a new vigor. Moreover, his song choice was more inspired than it had been in two decades, as he delivered the goods on such gems as Billy Joe Shaver's *The Cowboy Who Started the Fight*, John Prine and Steve Goodman's *The Twentieth Century Is Almost Over* and Kris Kristofferson's *The Last Time*.

Still, the album produced no hits and little sales, though Columbia certainly must take some of the blame on this one — with country music amid a revival, Cash should have connected with the young punk rockers and new-wave kids then energizing rock 'n' roll. But it would take another 15 years before a record company would understand how to connect Cash with a younger audience.

He was no longer the hottest artist in town, but he remained an icon to young and old alike — even if radio wouldn't give him a chance anymore. In fall 1980, Cash received the greatest honor given to a performer in his field — he was elected to the Country Music Hall of Fame. He was the first living person inducted into the hall.

When he accepted his honor, he made a comment that seemed pointed at how formulaic and predictable country music had become. "Many can sing country music, but not many *are* country music," he said. "It's the stylists that have made country music what it is today and given music a shot in the arm. So do it your way. Don't let yourself get caught in a bag."

Later, he would reflect back on the hall of fame as the greatest honor he achieved.

"I've been given all kinds of awards in my career, before and after 1980, including some big ones — Grammys, the Kennedy Center Honors, the Rock 'n' Roll Hall of Fame — but nothing beats the Country Music Hall of Fame, or ever will," he wrote in his autobiography.

Next, he went into the studio with Columbia Records executive Billy Sherrill, who was enjoying success with great records by George Jones. But Sherrill's dramatic sense of style and orchestral grandeur was a mismatch for Cash, who works best in simpler settings. The resulting album, "The Baron," sneaked in a Top 10 song in the title cut, but the album wasn't a success commercially or creatively. "We were both pretty cynical," Cash said of the outing.

"We certainly didn't give it our best. 'The Baron' flopped and the situation between me and CBS deteriorated."

After minor eye surgery in 1981, the doctor prescribed Cash pain pills to take until the effects of the operation waned. But there was a problem: The pain stopped long before he stopped taking the pills. Then, before this situation could be remedied, Cash had a nasty run-in with an ostrich that required a longer stretch of pain pills.

Johnny and June had filled their vast land with exotic animals, including peacocks, llamas, wild boar, buffalo and ostriches. In the winter of '81, a terrible cold spell hit Middle Tennessee and the ostriches took it hard. Several froze to death. One day, as Cash was walking along a trail on the land, he met up with an angry ostrich. Until then, he'd always been able to walk among them, without fear or confrontation. But this one seemed hell-bent on attacking him. The bird ruffled its feathers, made a ghastly hissing noise, then charged him. Cash had a walking stick and took a swing but missed. But then, the bird leapt high, then came down with its talons zeroed in on Cash's body. The attack and fall sliced deeply into his stomach and broke five ribs. Justified in taking pain pills, Cash took more than he needed. He started pirouetting through doctors again, getting pills from all of them without telling any of them about the others.

When the pills upset his stomach, he started drinking to kill that pain. Then he added amphetamines — his old nemesis — to his daily concoction. They gave him a lift when the pain pills lowered his energy. Now he was pain-free, full of energy — and addicted again. He even had bleeding ulcers brought on by all the abuse, but it didn't slow his intake.

While high one night, he tore up his hand trying to pull an imaginary Murphy bed from a hotel wall. All he pulled down was some paneling, nails and splinters, which damaged his hand. He left it untreated and it became badly infected, which forced him to check into Baptist Hospital — and ask for stronger pain medicine. Meanwhile, he hid a stash of Valium, Percodan and speed pills.

By the time his hand was operated on, the doctors discovered the internal bleeding caused by his ulcer. So another surgery took out part of his stomach and spleen. He hid his stash of Valium in the thick gauze dressing over his stomach wound. Days later, when medical personnel couldn't figure out why they couldn't keep Cash awake, they finally discovered the culprit: The Valium had dissolved in the dressing and was dripping down into his stomach through the wound.

This time, his family treated his addiction in a more modern fashion: They organized an intervention. With help from a doctor from the Betty Ford Clinic in California, his family arrived en masse one day at his hospital room. His mother Carrie, his wife June, his daughters Rosanne, Cindy and Tara, his son John Carter, his stepdaughter Rosie, his band, his household staff — about 25 people total.

Each wrote a message to him, each full of the pain of dealing with an addict. The toll piled up, all the lies, betrayals, disappointments, neglect, abandonment, fear and pain that he created in those he loved the most. The letters also expressed love toward him and they encouraged him to help himself and to seek assistance in healing himself.

Cash agreed, willingly and eagerly, to enter the Betty Ford Clinic. Once again, he came out on the other side of addiction — recovered, refreshed, reborn and back in love with life, his family and his music. "I know now why I am the way I am, that chemical dependency is a disease," Cash said. "And I know it's a progressive disease. The second time around, I went down lower and hit the bottom harder than I'd ever imagined was possible and if there's a next time it'll be even worse."

Cash began talking publicly about it, too, both to let people know what he went through and to encourage others to seek help if they needed it. "I could blame my mother for the fact that I'm an addict or I could talk about all the pressure I'm under. But that wouldn't be honest. I was in the supermarket the other day, watching one of the checkout girls bagging groceries and I thought to myself: 'Cash, that girl right there is probably under more pressure right now than you've ever been,' " he said. "It's simple: I'm an addict because I really like drugs."

So it came time for him to face the facts. But in doing so, he came up with another reality of drug recovery: Just because you learn the hows and whys, and even though you feel better and realize how bad they are for you, it doesn't mean the desire stops. "I want drugs every day and I think I always will," Cash said in an interview with *Country Music* magazine. "I've that wild streak, that black dog inside me that wants to bite. So choosing not to take drugs is a daily thing. I have to watch my flanks. Some mornings I have to sit quietly and say to myself: 'At this particular point in the day, Cash, you're going to be tempted, 'cause you're going to be seeing so-and-so and he's gonna have a drawer full of the stuff, so just before you get there, you start thinking about the Betty Ford Center.' Ugh! That works."

Cash also started talking daily to his old party buddy, Waylon Jennings, who was now free from drugs as well. "Addiction is progressive, but so is sobriety. The more time goes by, the better I feel. The better life is. Now I'm so happy at home with June and John Carter. I can't wait to wake up in the morning. I didn't used to wake up. I'd come to when the drugs wore off. I dreaded the light of day when it cracked through those windows. I'd have to pull the covers over my head, go take something else to make me sleep a little deeper. But now I'm up at 5:30 or 6, and I love my quiet time in the morning. I'll have my coffee. I'll read the Bible. I'll sit in front of the TV with the sound off and reflect on the day coming. Sometimes I'll make a list of things I want to do, even things I want to think about. And I'm much more productive these days."

19

On one of his regular concert tours of Europe, a spontaneous reunion with several old friends led to a one-of-a-kind live album that no one planned. Cash and his band were performing in Stuttgart, Germany, at the same time that Carl Perkins and Jerry Lee Lewis had a night off in the same city. Perkins and Lewis decided to attend the show and when Cash realized they were in the auditorium, he invited them to perform at the start of the second half of the program.

The trio stayed for an entire set, performing each other's hits, joining together on old gospel classics like *I'll Fly Away* and *Peace In the Valley*, and jamming on standards from the American songbook, such as Gene Autry's *Silver-Haired Daddy of Mine* and *Goin' Down That Road Feelin' Bad*. Certainly an unforgettable night for those in attendance, the special night also was caught on tape. The trio polished it up a bit and released it as an album, "The Survivors Live." A special, one-of-a-kind event, it captures three veterans enjoying themselves without the pressure of doing anything more than having a good time.

The Cash family dealt with one of the most frightening events in their lives on Christmas evening 1982. They were at their Cinnamon Hill home in Jamaica, as usual, on the holidays and they had brought a crowd with them. Besides Johnny, June and John Carter, the guests included Johnny's sister Reba, her husband Chuck Hussey, three members of their household staff plus their cook's stepdaughter, archaeologist Ray Fremmer and John Carter's young friend Doug Caldwell.

At the time, the Cashes didn't keep a security staff and they left the doors unlocked. That would all change after this particular night.

They were sitting for Christmas dinner at the long dining table when three men rushed into the house through three different doors. They all were wearing stocking masks and each had a weapon — a knife, a hatchet and a pistol.

As Cash described it in his second autobiography, the thieves first words were: "Someone is going to die here tonight!" One of the maids fainted immediately. The invaders demanded a million dollars. Cash explained, as calmly as he could, that they weren't allowed to bring that large of an amount of money into the country.

It was a desperately frightening night and many of the women — especially Reba, June and one of the maids — reacted hysterically at times. June thought she might be having a heart attack, as did the housekeeper who passed out. Reba bawled as the young attackers dragged them from room to room, the pistol pointed to 11-year-old John Carter's head and took all the money, jewelry and valuables that they could find and haul off. When the three robbers ordered everyone to the basement, some of the women thought for sure they were all going to be killed. But the thieves locked them in and left, then returned and slid a plate of turkey under the door for everyone to share. Then they took off.

Jamaican police killed the oldest of the robbers that night. The other two were later arrested and shot in prison. Cash, reflecting on the incident in his book, said he wasn't sure how to feel about how the men were dealt with. "My only certainties are that I grieve for desperate young men and the societies that produce and suffer so many of them and I felt that I knew those boys. We had a kinship, they and I: I knew how they thought, I know how they needed. They were like me."

Despite many recommendations and the fear of his family and friends, Johnny refused to sell his Jamaican home or give up his vacations there. He did add around-the-clock armed security on the perimeter. And, from then on, they locked their doors every evening as darkness fell.

In 1983, Cash returned to the studio with Brian Ahern, who by then was divorced from Emmylou Harris. This time the sessions created something more enduring and the resulting album, "Johnny 99," stands with "Rockabilly Blues" as Cash's best album of the era. The song selection was outstanding, including two Bruce Springsteen covers (*Highway Patrolman* and the title cut) that were perfect for Cash's portentous tone. Other songs were just as strong, however, including Cash's versions of Guy Clark's *New Cut Road* and two songs by British songwriter Paul Kennerley, who had just moved to Nashville — and would soon become Emmylou Harris' next husband.

By now, with country music in another cyclical upswing, Cash looked as if he was on a creative roll. He followed a couple of excellent albums — "Johnny 99" and "Rockabilly Blues" — with yet another solid effort, "Rainbow." Again, the success came for simple reasons: well-selected songs and simple yet musical arrangements that played to Cash's strengths. The material fit Cash's age and bearing: Philosophical tunes like Kristofferson's great *Here Comes That Rainbow Again*, Gail Davies' profound *Unwed Fathers* and a cover of John Fogerty's *Who'll Stop the Rain* all stand up well with the gravity and grounded power that Cash gives them.

In the liner notes to "Rainbow," Cash described what keeps him excited about music and creating albums. "Every once in a while a song comes along for me that gives me a boost," he wrote. "This has been the key to my continuing to enjoy performing after 30 years. I forget the miles and the years, and that song and I become one."

Almost simultaneously, he received a career boost with the release of the first Highwaymen album, the collaboration between Cash, Willie Nelson, Waylon Jennings and Kristofferson. The title song, Jimmy Webb's *Highwayman*, became the first No. 1 hit for Cash in nearly a decade.

The idea came about when Cash did an ABC-TV

Christmas special and he invited Willie, Waylon and Kris to join him. "We had so much fun," Cash said, "we decided to make a habit of it."

Cash and Jennings had the most history, going back to the time in the mid-'60s when they roomed together — and when Jennings encouraged his friend to buy a house of his own in the Nashville area. They had remained buddies ever since, always supporting each other as they battled to hold onto their distinctive styles and sounds while working within the Nashville music system.

Jennings first met Kristofferson after the songwriter left his post as an Army captain and moved to Nashville to pursue songwriting. Kristofferson was cleaning the CBS Studios when Cash recorded albums there in the late '60s. Cash was one of Kristofferson's heroes, and Johnny resisted Kris' aggressive advances at first — throwing him off his property after that helicopter stunt.

But once Cash paid attention, he recognized Kristofferson's genius. "Since his talent was revealed to me, I don't think I've performed a single concert without singing a Kristofferson song," Cash has said. "*Sunday Morning Coming Down* is the one people identify with me most strongly, but if I had to pick the one I love best, I think it would be *Rainbow*. In fact, that might be my favorite song by any writer of our time.

Besides all that, Kris is kind and funny and honorable; he stands up for his beliefs and he won't let you down."

Cash didn't really know Nelson before they formed the Highwaymen. Willie had long been close to Waylon and Kris, so they did have some friendly ties. Cash described him as "very perceptive and precise, and often very funny. He has a beautiful sense of irony and a true appreciation for the absurd. I really like him."

The quartet also staged a highly successful international tour, traveling the country with their wives and families along with such old friends as guitarist Marty Stuart and harmonica player Mickey Raphael. It was a taxing but fulfilling tour and they all played to larger crowds than they'd seen in some time. "Four for the price of one," Cash liked to say.

On stage, they looked like the Mount Rushmore of American music, four craggy-faced veterans who earned every line in their faces. Altogether, they'd survived 12 marriages, more than 115 years on the road and an endless amount of whiskey and pills. But by now they mostly had their wild times behind them. They were more likely to talk about their families than their parties or escapades.

"There is something warm and good about this tour," June Carter Cash said. "You can tell they're

friends and that they are having fun. I also see
survivors and it almost makes me cry. I want to
say, 'Thank you, God.' They've all been through
hell and fire water. But I always knew they'd be all
right because I think God touches certain people.
He gives them the talent and the experience so
that they can help other people with their music,
help heal the heartbreaks and lift the spirit."

"Being in a cowboy band is a way of getting
through life without having to give in," Jennings
said of the idea that all four members of the
collective had rebelled against the system in
their own ways. "None of us was interested in
just getting ahead. I didn't see why a country
singer couldn't do a Beatles song as well as a
Hank Williams song, and Johnny and Willie and
Kris all felt the same way."

Cash worked on another joint album, this time
collaborating with his old Sun Records cohorts,
Jerry Lee Lewis, Carl Perkins and Roy Orbison.
They cut their "Class of '55" album in Memphis
at Sun Studios and John Fogerty, Rick Nelson
and Marty Stuart also contributed. Fogerty wrote
the album's final song, a chugging boogie called
Big Train (From Memphis) that honored the
singers' contribution to American music.

The sessions allowed these legends to reflect
back upon what they had gained. All emerged
from dirt-poor backgrounds — Cash from

Arkansas, Lewis down the river in Louisiana, Perkins in Tennessee and Orbison in Texas. They all came to Sam Phillips, who gave opportunities to impoverished singers who likely wouldn't have been given a chance anywhere else. Sam loved music with a driving rhythm and the more he recorded it, the more he realized that this music — the sound of poor Southern blacks and whites — deserved more attention and access.

"From the Depression to World War II, there was so much in common between the black man's music and the Southern white poor man's music, between Jimmie Rodgers and Robert Johnson, and between Muddy Waters and Bill Monroe," Phillips said. "I recognized that, not because I was so smart, but because I enjoyed these kinds of music. Instead of the differences between them, I could see the likenesses. And I could see what was missing in both. Together, I thought they could be stronger."

After Elvis Presley's success at Sun, young men like Lewis, Cash and Perkins arrived at Phillips' door, looking for opportunity. He recognized what made them special. He didn't see their faults or see how raw and unformed they were. He heard their talent and recognized their natural charisma. He gave these guys a chance where others might have sent them on their way.

"You have to remember that the poor Southern

farmer was treated disrespectfully by the comfortable white classes, too," he said. "These men all understood the loneliness and hunger that poor whites and poor blacks had in common. Right up to the day they showed up on my doorstep, they were outcasts. They felt inferior, like poor people always have, but they were proud men, too. They came to Memphis because, after Elvis, they thought they might have a chance to sing their music and tell their stories."

Now, back in Phillips' studio again, they all had a chance to consider how much their lives changed because of their success. They also could look upon the changes they helped bring about to American entertainment and culture. For when they started, they were truly a part of a revolution.

"All of a sudden people from the poorest places in America were on the radio and eventually on television," Phillips said. "It was the first time poor people had a real voice, the first time they were making the most popular music of America. You can't comprehend now how important this was. I'll tell you, it unequivocally changed our culture. It caused social revolution, started moving us toward civil rights and all that. By God, it changed the world! That's the truth and can't nobody change it."

In the Memphis sessions, they returned to the

music that had brought on those changes. The songs they cut in that studio — Lewis' *Whole Lotta Shakin' Goin' On*, Perkins' *Blue Suede Shoes*, Cash's *I Walk the Line* and *Folsom Prison Blues*, Orbison's *Ooby Dooby* — will remain part of America's cultural fabric forever. This time, their recordings would be cut by Chips Moman, a veteran Memphis record producer who had a big hand in Elvis Presley's late '60s comeback.

In 1986, Cash finally published his long-worked-on novel, *A Man in White*, which covers a six-year period of the life of St. Paul. It was Cash's second enormous creative work based on a religious figure. He got the title from a vision St. Paul had on the road to Damascus, which was the turning point in Paul's life and the event that led him toward being a disciple of Jesus. Billy Graham played a major role in encouraging Cash to finish the book, convincing him to pick it back up and complete it after he had set it aside.

"I just got excited about getting it finished," he said. "My interest in Paul came back and I wanted to complete it. I'd always been fascinated with Paul's conversion on the way to Damascus. It started coming to me what this man was up against — to take the gospel of Jesus Christ into a world that already had more gods than they needed or could even remember. He had a very, very tough selling job."

Cash's job of writing the book got tough at times, too. "It took me a long time, years and years, during which my energies focused for a spell, then went somewhere else — music, drug abuse," he wrote in his second autobiography. "But I kept at it and eventually I finished it and got it published."

But, once it was out, he was proud of it. He worked as hard on the book tour as he usually did on his music tours. "I think maybe some Christians will like it and I hope some people who are not religious will like it, too," he said on his book tour. "It has its moments. I'm satisfied with it, but that doesn't make me a novelist."

Also in '86, Cash's long-running contract with Columbia Records came to an end. Prior to the '80s, country legends could count on staying with the same record company for decades — often for their entire careers. Cash, as famous as any star of his time, helped build Columbia into a powerhouse and he had sold more records for the label than any other country singer. So it shocked Nashville and the music world when word got out that Columbia would not renew Cash's contract. The uproar shook Nashville, a town not accustomed to controversy. Some industry insiders stormed Columbia's Music Row headquarters and pounded on the desk of Rick Blackburn, the head of the label's country division. Dwight Yoakam, then a new and up-and-coming star, blasted Blackburn and CBS Records for ditching a star whose royalties built their building and paid their six-figure salaries.

But Cash says he understood and was ready to go. He all but forced their hand by putting out an embarrassing novelty song called *Chicken in Black*, which included a video where the Man in Black is dressed in a chicken suit. The whole endeavor seemed humiliating — and far below a star of such magnitude and dignity. Cash told Blackburn, "You did what you thought you were supposed to do. I've always enjoyed working with you and I like you."

20

For many, the release of Cash from Columbia indicated the kind of drastic changes the country music industry was undergoing. Nashville no longer owned the power to make its own decisions; as record companies became more corporate-controlled, there was more pressure and more involvement from the headquarters in New York and Los Angeles. If an artist — old or new — went through a slow sales period, they often weren't given a chance to recover.

"The main thing for record companies right now is that they have to sell records," an executive from another record label said after Cash's release. "The longevity of country artists is greater than any other in the music business. But sooner or later, it's going to happen to Willie Nelson and Kenny Rogers. There's going to come a day when even they don't sell records." Another executive said, "It's like any other business. If you have people who aren't productive working for you, you get rid of them and find someone who can do the job."

Country record companies began targeting younger listeners in the '80s. As they signed younger singers, they noticed sales went up; so much of their concentration went into developing attractive, young singers who came across well on video, which was still a new marketing form at the time. "I guess I'm not pretty enough anymore," Cash cracked. "There are some really pretty people in country music now."

Cash realized that the company no longer felt eager to represent him and he no longer felt in touch with what they were doing as a company. "They had their new artists they were all excited about and I needed to go with someone who was excited about me, who thought I still had potential."

Not long afterward, though, he would admit in interviews that he felt out of touch with the Nashville record business and the changes it had undergone. Now artists were expected to court and politic their executives, to come to meetings, to lobby for creative direction, to coordinate and consult with the company about their albums and their artistic decisions. Cash refused to participate.

"I live out in Hendersonville, away from town, and I refused to come downtown to join in the fight: in the cutting of throats, sit in on the meetings, court this executive or that executive," he said. "For a long time there, I'd record an album and turn it in without even asking them what they wanted from me. I thought that if I did what I felt was right for me and turned it in, they should just go with it — but maybe I was expecting a little too much. And, as it turned out, album after album, it wasn't what they wanted. I saw the light when I did my dream gospel album; 20 songs I like to sing and feel good about. I finished it, turned it in and they rejected it."

His first move was to take advantage of his independence and give the album to Christian music industry label, Word Records. The two-record collection, "Believe in Him," surveyed old hymns and some new, original gospel recordings. "I've always wanted to do this album," he said in a Word Records press release announcing the album. "I've been hoping and praying for a record company that understood the gospel side of the record business to let me make an album like this. Word cares about gospel music and knows how to select and market the right songs and material."

MCA Records, one of Nashville's hottest labels at the time, passed on a chance to sign Cash as well. So he signed with Mercury/Polygram, at the time a minor Music Row player, but a major label nonetheless. The company was being restructured by promotion man Steve Popovich, a true music lover who leads with his heart more than his profit margin. Popovich, who worked for Columbia in the past, jumped at the chance to make Cash the fledgling label's biggest name.

Dick Asher, then the president and chief executive officer of Polygram in America, announced: "We are greatly pleased to begin this new association with a man of Johnny Cash's stature. His talents speak for themselves."

Popovich wanted Cash to make the kind of record *he* wanted; for the first time in a long while, the record company left the singer to his own devices. Popovich also called Cash every week, checking in on him, to chat. The Man in Black felt wanted for the first time in a long time.

Cash naturally reunited once again with Jack

Clement, his old Sun Records crony. His first Mercury album, "Johnny Cash Is Coming to Town," may be his most under-rated album. Sounding like he has something to prove, Cash corrals some great material — Elvis Costello's *The Big Light*, Guy Clark's *Heavy Metal* and a duet with Waylon Jennings on *Let Him Roll*. It's a consistently strong album that should have provided the singer with a commercial comeback. Unfortunately, it, too, was just as ignored as his Columbia albums had been.

"Water From the Wells of Home" paired Cash with several others, from Paul McCartney to the Everly Brothers to Emmylou Harris. The material was good, including a new McCartney song written just for Cash called *New Moon Over Jamaica*. The ex-Beatle wrote the song on the front porch of Cash's Jamaican home, Cinnamon Hill. McCartney, his wife Linda and their children came for Christmas dinner. Afterward, they sat outside and Paul wrote the song with everyone gathered around.

The album began as another Cash solo project. But early in its creation he recorded a duet with June Carter Cash called *Where Did We Go Right* and another with son John Carter Cash on the title track, *Water From the Wells of Home*. At that point, Cash remarked, "It took a turn toward family and friends."

So he called his old pal Waylon Jennings, who joined him for *Sweeter Than the Flowers*, an uncharacteristic song for both of them. His godson Hank Williams Jr. came in to cut *That Old Wheel*, a rollicking bit of philosophy that became Cash's favorite cut on the album. Hank Jr.'s blustery approach seemed to light a fire in Cash, who sings with a youthful, animated passion to match that of his friend.

When Emmylou Harris accepted the invitation to do a duet with Cash, she suggested a Roy Acuff song, *As Long As I Live*. It makes for a beautiful song that shows off Harris' wonderful talent for harmony vocals. He also recorded a Celtic song, *A Croft in Clachan*, with Glen Campbell and he revived his '50s hit, *Ballad of a Teenage Queen*, with harmonies by his daughter Rosanne and his friends the Everly Brothers.

Teenage Queen was the first single, most likely because Rosanne had just enjoyed a No. 1 hit with her cover of her Dad's old hit, *Tennessee Flat Top Box*. But the single failed, sounding a bit out of date for the time period. It kept the album from getting more attention. It failed to sell and the company did little to invest in promoting it.

Cash, aware that the album wasn't doing well, made apocalyptic announcements to the press. "I don't know. This might end up being my last album, I'm not sure," he said. "That's why I got all my friends and family together in the studio to sing with me — just in case."

Despite how poorly his records sold, Cash's profile was on the rise. He hosted a segment on the popular late-night comedy program, *Saturday Night Live*, and he played to a young crowd of rock fans at New York's trendy The Ritz nightclub, which earned him press raves.

The enthusiasm of young crowds struck him especially strongly. "They were so exuberant and carried away that I got to feeling really good," Cash told *USA Today*. "I enjoyed it more than I enjoyed playing Madison Square Garden in 1970."

To capitalize on his appeal to youth, Mercury executives suggested an album that paired the singer with hot rock stars of the time. Their initial ideas included U2, John Cougar Mellencamp and Bruce Springsteen. Cash, however, nixed the idea.

"I have no illusions about who I am and how old I am," he said. "Even though something at the Ritz might be a real big thrill, I know who my record buyers are. They're solid, dyed-in-the-wool country fans. Besides, I'm not going to bug those guys to record country music with me."

The next album, "Boom Chicka Boom," was another good one. Cash was writing better than he had in years, providing such fine songs as *The Backstage Pass, Farmer's Almanac* and the environmental protest song, *Don't Go Near the Water.* Elvis Costello contributed a fine original, too — *Hidden Shame*, written just for Cash.

By the time Cash released his last Mercury album, "The Meaning of Life," he'd lost his drive and the company completely backed out on supporting him. The album was inconsistent, though it featured some good material. But it barely made it out of the company warehouses.

Meanwhile, their Jamaican mansion sustained some damage from Hurricane Gilbert. In truth, the home was nearly indestructible. The limestone building has a specially designed windbreak, built in the shape of a round-edged, slope-roofed wedge. When the storm winds pound it, the wedge directs the force over the top of the structure. "It's very effective," Cash said, "and as far as I can tell, it's unique. I've never seen another like it anywhere in the world." The Cashes took two carpenters with them for Christmas to make repairs to the damage.

Just as the Country Music Hall of Fame inducted Cash during a lull in his career in 1980, the Hall of Fame center decided to feature Cash in a major exhibit at a time when his career once again was gasping for breath.

Opening in April 1988, the $70,000 exhibit included photographs, costumes, posters, film from early TV appearances, his guitars and such personal mementos as a Frederick Remington bronze sculpture. More than a million people saw the exhibit in the two years that it was displayed.

21

ohnny Cash almost died in 1988. He decided to visit Nashville's Baptist Hospital to check on his friend Waylon Jennings, who had just undergone heart bypass surgery. Waylon's doctor didn't like how Cash looked, so he suggested he undergo some tests. One artery was 90 percent clogged. The following day, Cash was admitted to the hospital.

Waylon came through his operation safely,

although he was weak. Cash asked him if it hurt. "Nah, it's not that bad, John," Jennings told him in a whispery voice. "By the time you wake up you won't feel a thing."

Cash went under the knife Dec. 19, 1988. He seemed to be recovering well when he got walloped by a case of double pneumonia. While on a respirator in critical care, he could sense his life slipping away. He heard the doctors and nurses shouting that he was crashing and everyone went into emergency revival mode. Cash later said he felt a light envelope him.

"It was the essence of light — a safe, warm, joyous brilliance growing brighter and more beautiful every moment," Cash wrote of the experience. "I began to drift smoothly into its very center, where it was so much better than anything I'd ever experienced that I can't possibly describe it. I was unbelievably happy. I've never felt such joy."

Then his heartbeat returned and he awoke to find himself being brought back by the medical staff.

Lying in his recovery room, his friend Waylon visited and Cash agonized over the pain, despite all the medicine he had been given. "It hurt like hell — really it was by far the worst pain I've ever gone through," Cash said. He confronted his friend about their pre-surgery pep talk, when

Jennings told Cash there wasn't much pain involved. "I know," Waylon said. "If I had told you the truth, I would've said you might as well go ahead and jump out of this three-story window and start running, because it would probably hurt less than going through a damn bypass operation."

In a January phone interview with writer Patrick Carr, Cash said, "I'm feeling really good. I still haven't got all my strength back. But it's only four weeks and four days since the surgery and I'm walking a mile and a half a day. There was still some fluid in my left lung three days ago, but it's gone now and my heart is just fine. My heart recovery rate — how long it takes for your pulse to get back to normal after exercise — is a third of what it was before the surgery. So, really, I'm in great shape."

By early February 1989, Cash received an A-plus rating from his doctors, according to a press release sent out at the time by his sister Reba Hancock of the House of Cash. "I have shed 18 pounds and I'm sticking with my diet," he said. "It's going great. My diet is wood and water and no tobacco. It's a matter of choices, either lust or life — and I choose life."

He also wanted to assure those concerned about how he was handling pain medication after all of his drug problems. He issued this statement: "For those concerned that the pain of this surgery would force me back to drugs, my answer is 'don't worry.' I am taking no medication."

The release went on to say that his doctors planned a timetable for easing him off the medication, "which has been accomplished," it said. Hancock added, "He looks better than I've seen him look in 10 years. He can't wait to get back on stage. In fact, his first scheduled appearance is in Jackson, Michigan, on March 11, just prior to an extended European tour."

However, eight months later, Cash announced he was entering the Betty Ford Center for "a refresher course." In a press release sent out by his manager Lou Robin, Cash said he had put off his stay at the Ford Center because of career obligations, but he finally cleared time in November 1989 for an extended stay: "Cash is not using, nor has he recently been using, mood-altering drugs. He is in excellent health. He has intended all year to go in for this relapse prevention therapy, but tour and recording schedules have not made it possible until this time. He entered the facility Nov. 19, 1989. He will remain there for a period of two weeks. He will resume his touring schedule in January 1990."

Johnny Cash's mother, the woman who told him that God's hand was on his shoulder, the woman who encouraged him to sing and to pursue it as a career, died in March 1991. For many years, his fans could find her running the counter at the House of Cash gift shop on Gallatin Pike in Hendersonville. Cash closed the souvenir shop after his mother's death.

In 1992, Johnny Cash was inducted into the Rock 'n' Roll Hall of Fame along with the Jimi Hendrix Experience, Sam & Dave, the Isley Brothers, Booker T. & the M.G.'s, Bobby "Blue" Bland and The Yardbirds. Although Cash admitted that it didn't equal getting elected to the Country Music Hall of Fame, he still considered it a great accomplishment — partly because he's primarily considered a country singer.

"It shows that rock 'n' roll knows its roots," Cash said. "And it shows that respect for people in one field of music toward those in another is a living thing. I think it was a tribute to the broader influence of country music on rock as well as an honor to me personally."

22

By 1993, Cash figured he was done making albums. He still toured and he did well with old fans eager to hear the legend sing his classics. He could have gone the rest of his days like that, just as fellow legends such as Jerry Lee Lewis or Chuck Berry had. He left Polygram Records and he felt no connection to what was going on in Nashville. "I feel like an outsider in this town," he said, "because they made me feel that way."

Meanwhile, country music was undergoing another youth movement. "The Garth Brookses and Alan Jacksons and Vince Gills have made life harder on older artists," radio program director Bob Moody said in 1993. "Too many program directors automatically dismiss their work without even listening to it."

Soon, however, Cash was visited from someone who *did* believe in him — a producer best known for rap and heavy metal. The producer showed intense interest in putting Johnny Cash back on record. At their first meeting, Cash didn't know what to think of this unconventional man.

Rick Rubin appeared in raggy, thrift shop clothes. His hair was past his shoulders, the top of his head was nearly bald and his beard grew past his chest because he had never trimmed it.

In a second meeting, Rubin told Cash what he had in mind: Johnny would just bring his guitar, they would set up in Rubin's living room and Cash could play the songs he loved — his own songs, other artists' songs, whatever. Rubin might suggest some, too, but only if Cash connected with them and felt comfortable presenting them. If they hit on something interesting, Rubin could record it. If they started to find a theme or an inspirational direction, they could follow it.

Cash, it turns out, had long dreamed of

making such a record. He saw it as an intimate album of just voice and guitar, singing quiet versions of some of his favorite tunes. He planned to call it "Late and Alone."

"So many producers have wanted to overproduce me like they've overproduced everybody else," he said. "The record companies and producers forget that my biggest-selling records are *I Walk the Line, Folsom Prison Blues, Ring of Fire* and *A Boy Named Sue.* They all had three, maybe four instruments on them." Rubin agreed with the concept and told Cash that there was no agenda other than to make music with passion that represented Cash at his best. "We'll just be totally honest," Rubin remarked.

"Rick Rubin's track record didn't really have a lot to do with my decision to work with him," Cash said. "I liked the way he talked about how he'd like to set me in front of a microphone with my guitar."

Cash signed with Rick Rubin's American Records in late 1993. It was the first step in a career revival that was unprecedented in modern American music. He completely committed himself to the project and ended up recording more than 100 songs in Rick Rubin's living room. At some point they experimented with adding instruments, but they decided it sounded best with just Cash and a guitar. The result was

Cash's strengths boiled down to their essence. Instead of trying to find a way to fit Cash's style into a modern context, as Nashville record companies kept doing, Rubin just helped the legendary singer make the best, most distinctive record possible. "The thing about it I loved was that Rick was trying to find out the heart of who I am as a musician," Cash said. "It's got me as excited as when I was 21."

The album, "American Recordings," immediately caused a sensation. It opened with an older song, *Delia's Gone*, initially recorded in the early '60s — and which he rewrote slightly to make it even more menacing than his original. The song finds a man recounting how he brutally killed his lover for cheating on him, then is haunted by her memory while wasting away in jail. Cash sounded more vital and more scary than he had in over 30 years. Rubin got exactly what he wanted. "He got the honest, unadulterated essence of Johnny Cash, whatever that is," Cash wrote of the record. The album won a Grammy Award for Best Contemporary Folk Album.

On tour, Cash found sold-out audiences who showed an exuberance and lust for his music that he hadn't seen since the '50s. The crowd was much younger, too, and they adored his every move and word. "I realized I'd come full circle, back to the bare bones of my music, pre-stardom, pre-electric, pre-Memphis," he wrote in his second autobiography. "I could have been back in Dyess, singing with just Momma to hear me on the front porch under the clear night sky of Arkansas in the 1940s with the panthers screaming in the bush and it seemed finally and almost miraculously that the audience enjoyed that feeling almost as much as I did."

Cash wrote some exceptional new songs for the album, too. *Drive On* comes from the point of view of a Vietnam vet, but it just as easily could be about an old road warrior like Cash. It begins by saying he's gone 25 years without getting his due, which is just about right. He talks of his haunted nightmares, of how his children love him but don't understand him and how well his woman knows him.

He could have been describing his own life. "*I was crazy, and I was wild,*" he sang, "*and I have seen the tiger smile. I spit in a bamboo viper's face, and I'd be dead but by God's grace.*" Every word of it was true.

Another song, *Thirteen*, comes from the darkest of the heavy metal singers and song-writers, Glen Danzig of the rock band Danzig. It's about a man born into bad luck and trouble who tattoos the number 13 onto his neck and Cash inhabits it with all the danger he can muster. Other songs came from such outstanding writers as Leonard Cohen, Tom Waits, Loudon Wainwright III and Nick Lowe.

Some critics wondered if Cash took on a rebel pose to appeal to rock fans — downplaying his recovery and the spiritual focus he maintained for the previous 25 years. "He's done a lot of work in Christian music, so when I think of Johnny, I think of him in those terms — not as some kind of rebel," said radio programmer Bob Moody.

But Rubin and American Records disagreed. "He's the original rebel and he has all that mystique of being the outsider and the loner," said an editor of a trade magazine that goes out to university radio stations. Rick Rubin agreed: "He's the quintessential image of rock 'n' roll, really — the outsider."

By the summer, Cash hooked up with the biggest rock 'n' roll event of 1993 — the Lollapalooza tour, which mixed underground and alternative rock acts with major heavy metal and punk rock groups. The headliner for that year's tour would be Nirvana.

Cash's daughter Rosanne didn't think he should do it. "I said, 'Dad, do you really want to do that? I would hate to see you in the position of playing to a bunch of snot-nosed 14-year-olds who don't really appreciate you.' But my father always told me that he could learn more from 19-year-olds than he could from people his own age."

At first, Cash himself didn't think Lollapalooza would be right for him. "My first reaction was to run," he said. "But then I got to thinking, 'Why not?' Young people especially see so much video and film that they know what's real when they see it. They appreciate the honest and open baring of emotions. And you can't have any more honesty than just taking a guitar up there and singing your songs."

The album not only revived Cash's career, it also reignited his passion for making music. That fire would continue to burn until his death.

For the last 10 years of his life, he was always making music, writing songs, thinking about the next recording session with Rick Rubin.

For their second album, Rubin and Cash both agreed that they should use a band this time, but keep the same formula: a few unexpected covers of songs by modern rockers, a couple of age-old gems and a couple of new Cash compositions.

For "Unchained," Cash worked largely with the rock group Tom Petty & the Heartbreakers. It still had a lean, mean sound to it, but was definitely fuller than the previous album. Cash covered songs by alternative rocker Beck (*Rowboat*) and hard rockers Soundgarden (*Rusty Cage*). He revived an old Carter Family song, *Kneeling Drunkard's Plea*, and wrote a poignant original, *Meet Me In Heaven*, a song directed toward his wife.

It would be a jarring juxtaposition, the hipper material rubbing against the religious tones. But Cash pulled it off because he has both those elements — the hip and the spiritual — upfront in his character. "The spiritual song on this album has Jesus mentioned practically every other word," Cash said in 1994. "But it took guts to do that, because that's what I do — I hear a good song, I don't hear what you wanna call it. To me it's a good song if I can sing it and make it my own. And *Meet Me In Heaven* — the title is carved into my father and my brother's tomb-stones and I've just always wanted to write a song called that. And yes, I do feel the power in gospel — that's what it's all about. They carry me away, those gospel songs."

23

Johnny Cash learned that he had a neurological or nervous disorder in 1997 when he almost died of double pneumonia. At first, he was diagnosed with Shy-Drager Syndrome, a sort of advanced form of Parkinson's disease. He spent 12 days in a coma at Nashville's Baptist Hospital. But once again he pulled through and his health improved. He woke from his coma when Merle Haggard came to visit. Haggard was rubbing his forehead to Cash's when the singer gained consciousness.

"I want to thank the people for being so nice to me," he said of the attention his hospital stay received. "I had so many people praying for me when I was really sick. The prayers were answered and I had a miracle of God that brought me up out of that bed. I didn't know that I'd been in a coma. I thought I'd had an overnight sleep. I woke up and asked for a cup of coffee and everybody started crying, praising the Lord. Everybody was around my bed. I said, 'What's everybody crying for?' One by one they would talk to me and tell me what had been going on, that people were holding a vigil all night long because they thought I was dying. Even my doctor was on her knees all night long. She said she told God she had done all she could do and it was up to him. Well, he brought me out of it. The prayers of the people got his attention."

June Carter Cash had only released one solo album in her career before "Press On," an idiosyncratic collection that her husband encouraged her to create. The idea for the album germinated when a Nashville record executive, Vicki Hamilton, saw June perform with her husband at Los Angeles' House of Blues in 1996. Hamilton sought June out to goad her into making an album of her own and to put it out on her own independent record label. Hamilton offered to put June into the most expensive studios of Los Angeles or Nashville, but the singer wanted something simpler.

"I told her that it's not the best studio, but that we had this little cabin and that it was where John recorded part of his album with Rick Rubin," June said. "It was just an idea I had, but once we got started, I realized just how important it was that we record it back here. This place is a part of us, a part of my family. And when I come out here, it takes me back, back to where I'm from. It's a very simple, very old place. And I like that. That's the kind of thing I like."

That spirit — rustic, primitive, simple, familial — winds throughout "Press On." Several of the songs were from the Carter Family repertoire, songs she sang before she could talk. "I wanted the first and last song to be Carter Family songs," she said. "Those are my bookends, because everything I'll ever do is framed by that. What's in between is basically who I am."

As for the title, she said, "It's something I've said all my life. No matter what happens in your life, good or bad, you have to keep moving on. I say that because I know, even in hardship, that I'm pressing on to a better life. That's where I'm headed and that's what this album is about. So it's a good name for it."

In her song *I Used to Be Somebody*, June looked back at her one-of-a-kind life by listing many of the famous people she knew well. Anyone who spent time in her presence realized that she wasn't just a friend of the celebrated; in person, she had as much charisma and personal force — indeed, as much star power — as the many legends she had nurtured and inspired. However, along the way, she undoubtedly collided with some of the most important cultural icons of her time.

I Used to Be Somebody tells of her relationships with Elvis Presley, Hank Williams, Patsy Cline, James Dean, Marlon Brando and playwright Tennessee Williams. All were more than casual acquaintances of hers before she even married Cash. The list could have gone on to include not just entertainers and artists but world political and religious leaders. That's just how June Carter Cash was — she had an impact on people's lives. It wasn't just the famous she comforted and cultivated, but a countless number of souls who crossed her path. She had the kind of open-hearted, energized warmth that pulled people in and made them feel special.

As the nation realized Johnny Cash's health was failing, people began lining up honors and re-assessing his career and his impact. Columbia began an extensive reissue program that included major collections (a new two-CD "Essential" album and a 3-CD set called "Love, God, Murder," breaking down his songs into those three categories). In June 1998, several young and veteran country stars toasted him with a tribute at Nashville's Ryman Auditorium. In February 1999, Cash received a Grammy Lifetime Achievement Award from the National Recording Arts & Sciences. Also in 1999, Turner Network Television staged an All Star Tribute to Johnny Cash at the Hammerstein Ballroom next to Madison Square Garden. An audience of more than 2,500 fans, including singer Michael Stipe of R.E.M. and film director Peter Bogdanovich attended the musical tribute.

Actor Jon Voight hosted the event, saying Cash created "some of the greatest music this country has ever produced, songs that speak of deep personal truths." The performances included everything from an acoustic rendition of the murder ballad *Delia's Gone* by hip-hop star Wyclef Jean to a roof-shaking take on Cash's old spiritual *Belshazzar* by the gospel vocal group Fairfield Four, who were joined by Marty Stuart. June Carter Cash sang her own composition, *Ring of Fire*, backed by her guitar, fiddle and her own autoharp playing. Other performers included Sheryl Crow, Kris

Kristofferson, Trisha Yearwood, Brooks & Dunn, Lyle Lovett, Emmylou Harris, Mary Chapin Carpenter, The Mavericks and Dave Matthews. Bob Dylan, Bruce Springsteen and U2 provided taped performances.

"I've known him since I was his janitor," Kristofferson said. "I've become his friend and have a son named for him. The strange thing is that the familiarity has never diminished his size. He still looks larger than life to me."

Introducing his version of *Give My Love to Rose*, Springsteen said, "You took the social consciousness of folk music, the gravity and humor of country music and the rebellion of rock 'n' roll and told all us young guys that not only was it all right to tear up all those lines and boundaries, but it was important."

Springsteen's performance proved especially moving to Cash. "That's always been one of my favorite songs that I wrote, but I never expected anybody else to sing it," he said. "I thought he did a really great job on the song." He also praised U2's reggae reworking of *Don't Take Your Guns to Town*, saying, "Their arrangement was really interesting as well. There were some really fine moments on that show."

Cash's health had been precarious for weeks and he wasn't sure if he could to travel to New York. "He didn't know whether he would go or not, and then he got feeling real good," June said the day prior to the taping. "He said, 'I'll sing if I feel like it, right at the last, but it'll feel real good to sit there and watch what everybody else does.'"

Late in the program, Cash walked on stage just as actor Tim Robbins read the dramatic liner notes to the album "Folsom Prison Blues." Cash had his black acoustic guitar strapped on and flung behind his back and, as the spotlight hit him, he turned and said, "Hello, I'm Johnny Cash." The crowd erupted into an extended ovation.

It was his first time on stage in more than two years and Cash obviously relished the moment. His band consisted of his oldest cohorts — Marshall Grant on bass, W.S. Holland on drums, Bob Wootton on guitar, Earl Poole Ball on piano and John Carter Cash helping out on guitar. Showing little sign of his ongoing illness, Cash started with *Folsom Prison Blues*, then followed with *I Walk the Line*. He started the evening look frail and weak; he ended it on stage, full of vigor and life.

Afterward, Cash admitted that he was more nervous about performing that night than he had been in decades. "I felt like I was somebody else or somewhere else," he said after returning to Nashville. "I don't know — it was really a strange feeling. I didn't know if I could do it or not. I didn't know if I could perform."

But as soon as he got on stage, he suddenly felt a burst of energy and confidence — as if he was in a very familiar place, and it felt right. "The feeling changed after about 10 seconds after *Folsom Prison* was kicked off," he said. "I was really hyper because I was so excited. I tried not to be too hyper, because it probably wouldn't be too good for my health to get too hyper. I really got excited and I tried to hold it down."

He also reflected on the idea of his songs being performed by such a wide array of stylists, some of whom seemed to have little in common with each other. "These songs of mine have always been known as country songs," he said. "But these rock stars are recording them. They're still the same songs. They reached other people of so-called other ilks, other kinds of music, but it's all the same. I don't see where there was any boundary there that I had to cross with it."

Cash felt so good afterward that he began planning to travel with June on a short road trip to promote her "Press On" album. "I may go in and sing a song with her on some of her shows," he said. "I'll be there and I may sing on one or two songs."

Released in 2000, the "Love, God, Murder" album made for one of the more inventive compilations of an extensive song catalog ever put together. Johnny Cash chose the songs and sequenced them. It was released both as a set and as individual albums on each topic. "The way they were put together shows the way the man's mind works," said a Columbia Records spokesperson at the time.

Each volume featured rare, unpublished photographs from Cash's own memorabilia. June Carter Cash wrote liner notes to the "Love" collection. Filmmaker Quentin Tarantino did the liner notes for the "Murder" CD. And U2's Bono put together the "God" liner notes.

"Johnny Cash doesn't sing to the damned, he sings with the damned and sometimes you feel he might prefer their company," Bono wrote. "Big John sings like the thief who was crucified beside Christ, whose humble entreaties had Jesus promising that night he would see paradise. Johnny Cash is a righteous dude and he keeps righteous company with June Carter Cash and the Carter Family, but it's the outlaw in him we love. The 'thief' who would break and enter your own heart, and leave you with a nagging question: '*Were you there when they crucified my Lord?*' "

The "Love" CD featured such classics as *I Walk the Line, Ring of Fire, I Still Miss Someone* and *Flesh and Blood* as well as lesser-known cuts *Oh, What a Dream, Happiness Is You* and *I Tremble For You.* On "God," the emphasis is Cash's gospel material, while "Murder" had *Folsom Prison Blues, Delia's Gone, Don't Take Your Guns to Town* and such rarities as *The Sound of Laughter* and *Joe Bean.*

24

Late in their lives, Johnny and June Cash's relationship was a testament to the ideals of faith and standing together through the fire. They worked together, traveled together, woke each morning together and rarely spent time apart in the last decades of their lives. "She's the easiest woman in the world for me to live with, I guess because I know her so well and she knows me so well," he wrote about her. "We've both found our place where we totally belong, in every avenue of endeavor."

In the liner notes for his 2002 album, "American IV: The Man Comes Around," Johnny started off with these words: "I am persuaded that nothing can separate me from my God, my wife and my music. Life is rich when I can come home, after hours in the studio ... and curl up to June Carter. That's when I give God a 'Thanks a lot, Chief.'"

Throughout his illness, June Carter rarely left her husband's side. She was always the nurturer without complaint. It extended far beyond her family — wayward souls, drawn to her by forces known and unknown, always found their way into her prayers. In her 1987 book, *From the Heart*, she revealed that her husband would wake up in the middle of the night, see her on her knees on the floor with hands clasped and ask, "Who is it now?"

Cash spoke glowingly of his wife throughout their lives. "It's like we fill each other's needs," Cash said in an interview just prior to their 30th wedding anniversary. "She's my companion, my friend. We talk about things we don't talk to anyone else about. We understand each other. Sometimes it's scary — we can almost read each other's minds. She's my rock, my anchor. She's always there."

In a 2000 interview, Cash was asked if his illness was a burden on his marriage. "Nobody could ever be a truer companion through the sickness than June has," Cash said. "We're closer now than we've ever been in our lives. We've seen a lot of them die and fall, seen great artists bite the dust, but she and I have fought together and fought for each other, and we're one."

Cash released his "American III: Solitary Man" album in October 2000. Like its predecessors, it won great praise, but his voice sounded weaker and more strained than on the previous American albums. His illness and age seemed more present in every word and breath. He brought in a lot of guests for the album this time, too. Tom Petty returned and he provides background vocals on his song *I Won't Back Down*, as well as on Cash's cover of Neil Diamond's *Solitary Man*. Sheryl Crow brings vocals to *Field of Diamonds* and accordion on *Wayfaring Stranger* and *Mary of the Wild Moor*. Merle Haggard sings on one of the best new cuts, *I'm Leaving Now*.

"The song is the thing that matters," Cash wrote in the liner notes. "Before I can record, I have to hear it, sing it and know that I can make it feel like my own, or it won't work. I worked on these songs until it felt like they were my own."

The album also included *Mercy Seat*, written

by Australian rocker Nick Cave about a man facing the electric chair. "The song does no more than call attention to the issue of the death penalty," Cash said. "I won't make a stand either way on it. I just wanted to call attention to some of the heartfelt gut emotions that come along with it."

He had hoped it would provoke listeners into thinking about the issue to come to their own conclusions. "I wouldn't be so presumptuous to say that my music can change the country," he said. "It's about touching emotions and reaching people's hearts and guts."

His statements also started sounding more and more like a man who made some kind of reckoning with himself and his Lord about his mortality. "On the question of youth and old age," Cash continued, "I wouldn't trade my future for anyone's I know. After all my experiences of the past and present, I know I can bring the best song I know to the sessions. The future is not questionable. For me it is a path of light. Lit by those I know, who enrich my life. The Master of Life has been good to me. He gives me good health now and helps me continue doing what I love. He has given me strength to face past illnesses and victory in the face of defeat. He has given me life and joy where others saw oblivion. He has given me new purposes to live for, new services to render and old wounds to heal. Life and love go on. Let the music play."

Meanwhile, Cash learned in the winter of 2000 that he was misdiagnosed with Shy-Drager Syndrome. He said all along that he didn't think his illness fit the symptoms and he was right, it turned out. "My doctor told me in November that if I'd had it, I'd be dead by now," Cash said. "She said, 'You're getting better, so you don't have Shy-Drager's. And you don't have Parkinson's.' I'm in better health than I have been in a year or two. I worked all day yesterday in my yard. I pruned my grapevines. I've got grapes and muscadines. I've got fig trees that the winter tries to kill, but I'm covering them with hay to protect them from the cold."

When Johnny Cash won the Grammy Award for Best Male Country Vocal Performance, he wasn't in Los Angeles to pick it up. He was released from Nashville's Baptist Hospital just hours before the program after spending more than a week suffering from pneumonia. It was his fourth hospitalization for pneumonia in three years. Cash's "American IV: The Man Comes Around" was released in November 2002. Through all the illnesses and hospitalizations, he kept busy, always collecting songs, writing new lyrics and working with Rick Rubin and with his son John Carter on his music. Now that he didn't tour anymore, all of Cash's creative energies were focused on albums.

"You never know where you'll find a good song," he said. "I've always got my ears open, now more so than ever." By this time, however, he had glaucoma so bad that he could no longer see well enough to read. He also regularly battled asthma, which played into his periodic bouts with pneumonia.

The first week of May 2003, June Carter Cash underwent surgery to replace a heart valve. Her recovery was promising until May 8, when she went into cardiac arrest. She was without oxygen for a period of time and was placed on life support. The situation was dire. Johnny Cash sent out a message, through e-mail and word of mouth, for friends and fans to pray for his wife at 10 a.m. on May 12. But by that time, her family already decided to take her off the respirator. June Carter Cash passed away at 5:04 p.m. May 15. She died with her family by her side.

Cash was pushed into the funeral in a wheelchair, his face blank with mournfulness. As he came into the funeral home, he rose painfully, with the help of family members and leaned over the open casket and looked into his deceased wife's face. Then he said goodbye.

Among those attending her funeral were actor Robert Duvall, actress Jane Seymour and songwriters Kris Kristofferson, Larry Gatlin and Billy Joe Shaver. Rosanne Cash, who delivered her eulogy, said she never heard June use the word "stepchild." She always used the term children for all of her clan, Johnny's and hers. "She always said, 'I have seven children,'" Rosanne said.

"In her eyes, there were two kinds of people — those she knew and loved, and those she didn't know and loved. She was forever lifting people up." She added, "My father has lost his greatest companion, his musical partner and his soul mate."

In the days that followed, she was recognized not so much for her career and her artistry — though she was both a major star and an enormous talent — but for a lifetime of meaningful relationships. It wasn't just the famous who showed up at her funeral or who asked to speak on her behalf. Regular folk from across the nation traveled to bid farewell to a friend, several getting up to tell stories about how she'd personally touched their lives.

One of the many Carter Family songs June loved to sing was *Will the Circle Be Unbroken?* To close her album "Press On," the last album she released in her lifetime, she recorded it the way she liked to hear it, markedly slower than the usual hand-clapping version familiarly known as a closing encore at festivals and special musical

gatherings. June sang it so that a listener could
recognize its mournfulness at the passing of life
as well as its celebration of the circle of life. The
lyrics begin with a family watching as its matriarch, its bastion of spiritual strength, passes by in
a hearse. "*Undertaker, oh, undertaker,*" she sings,
"*please drive slow, because that lady you are
hauling, oh Lord I hate to see her go.*" The song
goes on to say that "*there's a better home a-wait-
ing*" and the matriarch of the Cash and Carter
clans steadfastly believed that was where she was
headed. June Carter Cash believed that the love
she so generously gave, and the suffering she so
willingly absorbed, was all a part of the journey
leading her home.

Johnny Cash continued to work after his wife's
death. In fact, he spent almost every day considering songs — writing, arranging and planning
to record. He was deep in a flurry of work and
concentration, and those who saw him thought
he seemed fairly healthy. He was thrilled when
he was nominated for four MTV Video Music
Awards and he talked of attending the New York
ceremonies. "He was just enjoying it — the
whole process of making music," his old friend
Jack Clement said of his final weeks. "He put all
his energy into it. It was something for him to
look forward to. He said it was his therapy."

But then he came down with a stomach

ailment and was hospitalized Aug. 25. He left the hospital Sept. 9, only to be rushed back two days later. Johnny Cash died early on Friday, Sept. 12, from respiratory failure brought on by complications of diabetes. In his second autobiography, Cash said he wasn't afraid of dying. "I just don't have any fear of death," he wrote. "I haven't lost a minute's sleep over it. I'm very at peace with myself and with my God."

Dolly Parton, a longtime friend and fellow country music icon, said of his passing, "Johnny Cash has only passed into the greater light. He will never, ever die. He will only become more important as time goes by."

APPENDICES

AWARDS

Besides his scores of CMA, ACM and Grammy awards, Johnny had the distinct honor of being the only artist ever inducted into the Country Music Hall of Fame, the Rock and Roll Hall of Fame and the Songwriters Hall of Fame. His trophies have come from such varied places as the MTV Video Music Awards, where he won Best Cinematography in 2003 for his *Hurt* video, and the White House, where President Bill Clinton presented him with a Kennedy

Center Honor in 1996. In 1990, he became one of only a handful of country artists to receive a Lifetime Achievement Award from the National Academy of Recording Arts & Sciences. Here are highlights of some of the many honors he received.

INDUCTEE
Country Music Hall of Fame (1980)
Songwriters Hall of Fame (1989)
Rock and Roll Hall of Fame (1992)

CMA AWARDS
Johnny, who received 28 nominations and six wins in his storied career, won his first CMA on the inaugural telecast of the awards show in 1968. In 2003, 35 years after his first trophy, he was nominated for four awards, including Album of the Year for "American IV: The Man Comes Around."

Album of the Year ("Johnny Cash at Folsom Prison," 1968)
Entertainer of the Year (1969)
Vocal Group of the Year (with June Carter, 1969)
Male Vocalist of the Year (1969)
Album of the Year ("Johnny Cash at San Quentin," 1969)
Single of the Year (*A Boy Named Sue*, 1969)

GRAMMY AWARDS

Best Country & Western Performance Duet, Trio or Group Vocal or Instrumental (*Jackson*, 1967)

Best Country Vocal Performance (*Folsom Prison Blues*, 1968)

Best Album Notes ("Johnny Cash at Folsom Prison," 1968)

Best Male Country Vocal Performance (*A Boy Named Sue*, 1969)

Best Country Song (*A Boy Named Sue*, 1969)

Best Country Vocal Performance by a Duo or Group (with June Carter, *If I Were a Carpenter*, 1970)

Best Country Song (*Highwayman*, 1985)

Best Spoken Word or Nonmusical Recording (Interviews from "The Class of '55" Recording Sessions, 1986)

The Legend Award (1991)

Best Contemporary Folk Album ("American Recordings," 1994)

Best Country Album ("Unchained," 1998)

Lifetime Achievement Award (1999)

Best Male Country Vocal Performance (*Solitary Man*, 2000)

Best Male Country Vocal Performance (*Give My Love to Rose*, 2002)

ACM AWARDS
Single of the Year (*Highwayman*, 1985)
Pioneer Award (1990)

AMERICAN MUSIC AWARDS
Favorite Video Group ("The Highwaymen," 1985)

ON THE RECORD

The Man in Black recorded some 1,500 songs in an extraordinary career that spanned almost half a century. He charted 137 hits on Billboard's Country Charts, of which 52 landed in the Top 10. On the next two pages is a chronological list of these Top 10s — with stars next to his 14 No. 1s.

So Doggone Lonesome (1956)
Folsom Prison Blues (1956)
★ I Walk the Line (1956)
★ There You Go (1956)
Train of Love (1956)
Next in Line (1957)
Home of the Blues (1957)
★ Ballad of a Teenage Queen (1958)
Big River (1958)
★ Guess Things Happen That Way (1958)
Come in Stranger (1958)
The Ways of a Woman in Love (1958)
You're the Nearest Thing to Heaven (1958)
All Over Again (1958)
What Do I Care (1958)
★ Don't Take Your Guns to Town (1959)
Luther Played the Boogie (1959)
Frankie's Man, Johnny (1959)
I Got Stripes (1959)
Seasons of My Heart (1960)
In the Jailhouse Now (1962)
★ Ring of Fire (1963)
The Matador (1963)
★ Understand Your Man (1964)
The Ballad of Ira Hayes (1964)
Bad News (1964)
It Ain't Me, Babe (1964)
Orange Blossom Special (1965)
The Sons of Katie Elder (1965)

Happy to Be With You (1965)
The One on the Right Is on the Left (1966)
Jackson (1967)
Long-Legged Guitar Pickin' Man (1967)
Rosanna's Going Wild (1967)
★ *Folsom Prison Blues* (live version) (1968)
★ *Daddy Sang Bass* (1968)
★ *A Boy Named Sue* (1969)
Blistered (1969)
If I Were a Carpenter (1970)
What Is Truth (1970)
★ *Sunday Morning Coming Down* (1970)
★ *Flesh and Blood* (1970)
Man in Black (1971)
A Thing Called Love (1972)
Kate (1972)
Oney (1972)
Any Old Wind That Blows (1972)
★ *One Piece at a Time* (1976)
There Ain't No Good Chain Gang (1978)
(Ghost) Riders in the Sky (1979)
The Baron (1981)
★ *Highwayman* (1985)